SINS OF THE TONGUE

Sins of the Tongue

or

Jealousy in Woman's Life

Followed by Discourses on
Rash Judgments, Patience, and Grace

By
Monseigneur Landriot,
Archbishop of Rheims

Translated from the French by
Helena Lyons

With Preface by the Bishop of Kerry

Loreto Publications
Fitzwilliam, NH 03447
AD 2008

First U. S. Printing by
Thomas B. Noonan and Co.
19-21 Boylston Street
Boston Massachusetts 1872

Front Cover Image:
The Gossipers by John Anthony Puller, with kind permission from
the copyright owner, The New Baxter Society, all rights reserved.

Published by:

Loreto Publications
P. O. Box 603
Fitzwilliam, NH 03447
603-239-6671
www.LoretoPubs.org

ISBN: 1-930278-68-3

Printed and bound in the United States of America

TABLE OF CONTENTS.

Table of Contents.

Table of Contents.

Table of Contents.

Table of Contents.

Table of Contents.

Table of Contents.

PREFACE.

"To read good books" is one of the first pre-
scriptions that spiritual advisers give to those who
desire to correct bad habits, or to strengthen and
cherish habits of virtue. For the greater number,
thoughtful reading supplies the place of formal
meditation; and for many, who are incapable of
sustained reflection, it is more suitable and therefore more effective.

But how are we to choose our spiritual books?

Reading some of the works of the saints, we
tread the higher regions of mystic theology, which
tell of God's dealings with heroic souls, and of the
strange paths by which He leads them. Such books
are unintelligible to most readers, even to very holy
and enlightened souls, whom God leads by humbler
and safer ways. Misconception might render them
positively dangerous. They might cherish delu-
sions or foment spiritual pride.

A large portion of the ascetic library has been written within the walls of the cloister. We have volumes numberless which treat of *religious* perfection. From such books persons living in the world may learn much, because Christian perfection is, in all states, essentially the same, and the virtues which lead to it, though differing in some accidental forms of expression or practice, rest on the same principles, and create the same habits in the outer world and in the cloister. Yet there is a certain unreality in books which treat of a kind of life different from our own, and which are addressed to persons having other obligations. We have to say so often, — "This is not for me," that we are apt to extend too far the inapplicability of what we read.

Attempts have been made, as in the case of that great treasury of spiritual knowledge, "The Christian Perfection" of Rodriguez, to adapt such works to the use of persons living in the world; but there is always discomfort in reading abridgments. We do not easily understand partial utterances; we want the whole mind of the author.

Many spiritual books date from an older time. Again, though human nature is ever the same, and the Church, which strives to control and purify human nature, is ever the same, yet the tendencies

to evil are not always in the same direction. And
as the spiritual action of the Church will consist in
applying specific remedies to prevailing vices, the
character and scope of ascetic books will be found
to vary from age to age.

We want books suitable to the present time, and
to the present state of society. We want books
suitable to the circumstances of those who live in
the world. Those who live in the cloister are abundantly supplied. We want an ascetic theology
which will deal with the ordinary occupations of
domestic life, and teach how the whole may be sanc-
tified and harmonized with the divine maxims of the
Gospel. St. Francis de Sales did this in his day,
and though more than two hundred years have
elapsed since he wrote, his writings have all the
charm of freshness and reality. Quaintness of
style, and imagery borrowed from obsolete science
of the past, give additional zest to the moral doctrines which flowed in sweetness from his gentle
heart.

Mgr. Landriot, the Most Reverend Archbishop
of Rheims, has been doing the same good work for
our day. Though he has not yet passed the prime
of life, he has sent forth many volumes. They are
eminently *actual*, suited in style and matter to the
present time. There is all the earnestness and

vigor which stamp this fast-going age. Illustra-
tions are borrowed from the world we live in now,
from its physical science, its history, its machinery,
— from the social fabric of the nineteenth century.
The society he instructs is that in which we live;
and without seeking to reconstruct it to the model
of some impossible ideal or worn-out reality, he takes
it as it is, and he labors to correct, to purify, and to
refine it by the application of the rules of Christian
Ethics, — of morality based on the Gospel.   There is
an inexpressible charm in the use of Sacred Scripture throughout these works.   The inspired sentence comes like a flash of light, and in its unexpected adaptation we see a largeness of meaning
which we did not see before, as when looking at the
various facets of the diamond, we see in each a
fresh and varied brilliancy.   But what gives to Mgr.
Landriot's works their real value is his thorough
knowledge of the world and the world's ways.   It
has manifestly no secrets for him.   He has penetrated into its inmost recesses, and he lays bare the
innermost things of its daily life.

The work which Miss Lyons presents to English
readers in her excellent translation, "Les Péchés de
la Langue," has a usefulness commensurate with the
evil with which it deals.   St. James gives us the
measure of this evil, — "The tongue is a fire, a

world of iniquity. The tongue is placed among our members which defileth the whole body, and inflameth the wheel of our nativity, being set on fire by hell." [1]

It is also most worthy of remark what a large portion of the sapiential books of the Old Testament is devoted to the proper regulation of the use of speech. The many texts quoted by Mgr. Landriot are only selections from the various forms in which the Holy Spirit tells us how much wisdom consists in governing the tongue.

The analytic table of this volume lets us see at a glance the comprehensive treatment of the subject. The attentive reader will find that there is neither vagueness nor exaggeration in the rules laid down for the good use of speech. Ascetic theology, which aims at perfecting the soul, does not occupy itself with distinctions of the relative criminality of our actions. It moves the soul to the avoidance of all evil, to its utter purgation, and then leads upwards and onwards, through every degree of the steep ascent. Moral theology weighs our actions, examines their object, motive, and circumstances, treats them with the coldness of science, attaching to each its measure of guilt, as far as human reason,

---

[1] Ch. iii. v. 6.

enlightened by revelation can do. In these admirable Lectures Mgr. Landriot combines the work of the ascetic and moral theologian ; for, while exhibiting all the higher sanctions of the moral law, he carefully lays down, in each matter, the conditions of grievous sin, so as to guard against the danger of a false conscience.

We are convinced that an attentive perusal of these Lectures will, with God's grace, enlighten the soul on those secret springs of thought and feeling from which flows so much that is faulty in human speech. It will promote charity, peace, patience. It will foster prudent restraint, — the wisdom of silence. At the same time conversation, regulated as here prescribed, will be graceful and refined, will be a source of pleasure not followed by the pang of remorse, and will be the right use of one of the greatest powers God has given to man. The translator has proved her competency for the task she has undertaken by rendering into English another work of Mgr. Landriot's, "La Femme Forte," which has been favorably received. The translation is not unattended with difficulty. As Mgr. Landriot addresses himself to modern French society, his language has much of the idiom and expression which makes French eloquence of the present day differ from that through which we, in our early days, learned the language, and differ still more widely from the genius of the English tongue. But we may congratulate Mgr. Landriot on having found a faithful interpreter, who has preserved in her translation the tenderness, the warmth, and the vigor of the original.

✠ DAVID,

Bishop of Kerry.

THE PALACE, KILLARNEY,
Nov. 28, 1872.

TO THE

LADIES OF THE SOCIETY OF MERCY,

ESTABLISHED AT RHEIMS.

MY CHILDREN, — You have expressed a desire that I, your Archbishop, should continue at Rheims the society I organized at La Rochelle. My paternal affection for you induced me to accept an invitation which permits of my being of service to you — of pleading the cause of the poor, and at the same time of enlightening your minds by a series of instructions on the duties of Christian women.

We have already commenced this work of charity and apostolic ministry, and, thanks to your zeal and devotedness, it is now on the road of flourishing prosperity. I feel confident that our Lord will continue to bless it, and that every one will derive advantage from it, — the poor, the Ladies of the

Association, and, I would also add, their families; for a truly pious woman is, as the Scriptures tell us, the glory and the ornament of her house : she is its joy and its happiness.

The dedication of this volume to you is in my eyes a duty, and a pleasing one. It contains the Discourses you have already heard, and in which you showed yourselves interested. I should wish you to keep this book in remembrance of our meetings; for thus it will bring to perfection and perpetuate the abundant fruits obtained from the divine seed we have sown. Though a printed sermon may not have the same influence as a spoken one, yet the ear which once heard it can reawaken by the aid of memory what seems an inanimate letter; it can call up again those heartfelt tones and utterances which were more than once inspired by the audience themselves.

May all the souls to whom these Discourses may have done some little good — may all the readers to whom this book may suggest some holy thoughts — deign to pay me with the coin of a Christian heart, — with a prayer and a *memento* at the foot of the Altar! This souvenir of the heart, this tribute tendered by a grateful soul, has wings, swift and strong, which overleap in the twinkling of an eye all barriers of distance.

Rheims, October 13, 1869, on the Feast of St. Theresa, that great saint who traced, with such a firm hand, the broad enlightened paths of true piety.

✠ JEAN FRANÇOIS,

Archbishop of Rheims.

FIRST DISCOURSE.

AIM OF THE ASSOCIATION.

"What shall we do?"—ACTS ii. 37.

WHEN we are invited to become members of any society, to give our names to any enterprise, to set out on any journey, our first question naturally is — Whither are we going? What shall we do? What are the means for carrying out our plans? And after we have pondered these thoughts for some time in our minds, they begin to come forth to the light, and seem to lie in wait for us on our way, persistently requiring an answer.

Nothing can be more legitimate than this tendency of the human mind, for every intelligent being wishes to know the ends proposed to him, and tries to take a survey of the road on which he is about to travel.

I shall suppose, then, my children, that at this moment you all rise together, and collectively address to me this question — We have assembled here to-day in this church, in accordance with your wishes. What is to be the aim of our meetings? What shall we have to do? What new mission are you about to confide to us? We are quite ready to do all that depends on us to second the views and projects of our Archbishop; but there is a previous question which we wish to have answered, that is, "What shall we do?"[1]

My answer to this question is easily given, my children, because I have nothing and can have nothing to conceal. My words shall be as clear, simple, and straightforward as truth itself, and will also, I trust, be leavened by the tenderness of charity.

Once a month, then, we shall assemble together to join in prayer at the foot of the altar,[2] when I shall address to you a few brief words of exhortation, and we will learn together how to love and succor the poor.

I.

In the first place, we are to meet in this church once every month. I do not know if you have ever seriously considered the power which an Association possesses. Anything isolated is generally weak and impotent. A drop of water is nothing in itself; it is so quickly absorbed by the earth, that when it falls you scarcely perceive it; but let another drop, let many other drops unite together, and you have a tiny rivulet. Let that rivulet flow on to meet others, and you have a great river, on whose bosom large ships are floating, and whose strength in the hour of floods is so irresistible that it sweeps away all before it. Look at that slight piece of iron wire; it could not

---

[1] Acts ii. 37.
[2] This first discourse was preached on the 21st of March, 1868.

of itself sustain any considerable weight; but join it with other pieces, and twist them together until you have made a spiral cord, whose windings you can scarcely follow, and then, by means of it, you can support massive bridges, such as we see in Switzerland, uniting mountains, and forming roadways over which the heaviest burdens may be safely carried. Let us take another example, specially applicable here, in our own city. A man has some little capital, inconsiderable in itself. He meets a neighbor, whose purse also is but moderate; they agree to unite their means together. In a little while they contrive to induce other men with like notions to join them, until they make up a hundred. They then form a company and establish a house of business, which soon attains a good position, flourishes, and extends itself on all sides.

Such is the power of an Association in the natural order of things. You need not wonder that it should possess that same power in the supernatural. In the first place, it is a universal law; it prevails throughout all the material creation, and in nearly every instance the laws which govern the world of bodies and nature are merely an emblem of those superior laws by which the world of souls and the more elevated sphere of the Redemption are governed. Christ has given a special guarantee and consecration to this great truth when He said, "Where two or three are gathered together in My name, there am I in the midst of them."[1] A commentator on this text does not hesitate to add, "I am in the midst of them just as is the Holy Ghost

[1] St. Matthew xviii. 20.

between the Father and the Son, the link and the bond of the love of the Two." [1]

What a consoling hope these words give me! O my God! what wilt Thou not effect in the midst of this great number of holy and fervent souls assembled in Thy name to pray, and listen to tidings of Thee and of Thy chosen friends the poor. Not only wilt Thou be in the midst of them, but Thy graces, Thy love, and Thy benedictions will be in proportion to the number and the piety of those assembled here in Thy name. Thou wilt then be in the midst of us, O my God! and Thou wilt come with full hands, or rather with heart full and overflowing towards us. Thy spirit of love will rest upon these dear souls, as Thy Spirit once moved over the waters, and dropped therein the seeds of an abounding vitality. Within these walls will flow a current of divine electricity, deriving its source from the Heart of Thy Divine Son, setting souls on fire, and inspiring them with new life and ever-increasing fervor.

We shall not only meet together, my children, but we shall also pray and approach the Holy Communion together. United prayer is all-powerful; it caused St. Thomas to say, "That it was impossible for the prayers of a pious congregation not to be heard when all join together, so that of many they form but one soul and one mind." [2] It is like a bell in which there is a mixture of many metals. Before being fused together, each separate piece of metal gives forth but a dull sound, and the effect of the whole is inharmonious, but as soon as they have passed through the fur-

---

[1] Cornelius à Lapide, in St. Matt. xviii. 20.   [2] In St. Matt. xviii.

nace, there results a silvery, melodious tone, charming
the ear and elevating the mind, by recalling it to the
things of eternity. We shall then pray one for another. Do you pray for your Archbishop and spiritual Father; ask for him all those graces which are so
necessary in order to enable him to do good and bear
his burden — a burden all the heavier that so few
know its weight. I in my turn shall pray for you. I
shall offer up your wants and the wants of all those
who are dear to you upon this altar, and implore for
all — husbands, children, and every member of your
families — those spiritual and temporal favors which
our Lord loves to bestow on His chosen friends. You
must also pray for one another, and all these mingled
supplications and prayers will form one great cry to
pierce the Heart of God. And what will not be within your power to obtain when many of you have the
happiness of approaching Holy Communion together,
when our Lord Himself shall come to place at your
disposal the treasures of His love.

I have just now pointed out the reason why Catholic Associations for good works continue to live. Men
of the world oftentimes embark on enterprises and
form projects with the best intentions and all the
good-will of upright minds. But good-will is not
enough to insure perseverance. Difficulties arise, and
with them the discouragement attendant on every
earthly undertaking; and even if such discouragement did not exist, the lassitude inherent in human
nature would be sufficient to account for a collapse.
Good resolutions grow cold, the best laid plans fall to
the ground; and even if such a company should con-

tinue to exist, sustained by some worldly considerations, it will do no more than lead a languishing life,
devoid of energy and vigor. This is not to be won-
dered at. Such engines have no steam, and steam
is necessary in every good work. I speak of that
heaven-born fire whose provision is never exhausted,
because it is replenished as soon as it begins to cool.
Now all this is evidently beyond the powers of our
poor human nature. Strength from on high, whose
vital source can never fail, is requisite for all that is
to last. This is so certain, that even in a Catholic
Association where the members neglect to meet often
in order to consult and pray together, thus renewing
their fervor and keeping themselves under the guidance of heavenly influences, there comes a time when
zeal cools, and gradually lessens until the words of
the Apostle become applicable to them — "I know
thy works; that thou hast the name of being alive,
and thou art dead."[1] We shall therefore meet to
pray and receive Holy Communion together.

At each meeting I shall address a few words of instruction to you, which is my second answer to the
question of "What shall we do?"

II.

A Christian woman has a great mission to fulfil in
this world, but to do it thoroughly and well she must
know and understand all her duties. I have always
thought, speaking from a religious point of view, that
a woman has the power of doing either a great deal

---

[1] Apoc. iii. 1.

of good or a great deal of harm, both in her own family circle and in society. A woman of true and sincere piety, and who at the same time is courteous and intellectual, is the best missionary the Gospel has. God has endowed her with a power of gentleness and sweetness which, when blessed by Heaven, and guided by virtue, can effect wonders. The very presence of a woman who knows how to combine an enlightened piety with mildness, tact, and thoughtful sympathy, is a constant sermon; she speaks by her very silence, she instils convictions without argument, she attracts souls without wounding susceptibilities; and both in in her own house and in her dealings with men and things, which must necessarily be often rude and painful, she plays the part of the soft cotton wool we put between precious but fragile vases to prevent their mutually injuring each other. But if a woman be not well informed and intelligent in her religion, if she have not a sincere love of her duties, she may do a great deal of harm. She actually becomes a sort of repelling power, especially to men who are already irreligiously disposed; she wearies and disgusts them; she becomes the cause of the complaints we so often hear from worldly lips, that woman's piety is only another species of excitement; it is an amusement they offer to their imagination, and they use it as a cushion on which to lay the whims of their foolish minds, and lull themselves into forgetfulness of their real defects.

I shall follow here, my children, the plan which I pursued at La Rochelle, that of placing before you the whole series of your duties on the various points of Christian morality, in which your sex is specially concerned. I shall be ever happy to do justice to the many excellences of woman; to her tenderness of heart, to her keen intelligence, to her self-devotion; to all those admirable qualities which form part of her nature. But you must also permit me to speak the truth boldly about those defects which are inherent in everything human: I shall never flatter you, although I may often praise you, for well-merited praise is not flattery; flattery only exists where the praise is exaggerated or false. Whenever I praise you, then, it shall be without flattery; and when I have to speak unpalatable truths, they will, I trust, be ever tempered by the circumspection of charity, and you may feel assured that they will always be dictated by a heart paternally devoted to your own dearest interests.

At these monthly homilies, or more truly speaking, these outpourings of my heart, I shall speak simply and with the freedom of a father. I shall enter into details, and while seeking to avoid vulgarity of speech, I shall still not shrink from using the unstudied language of the father of a family, who does not pause to weigh his expressions according to the studied rules of oratory. A father's heart needs free expansion, particularly when he is amongst his own children, and when he is addressing himself to daughters already disposed to listen indulgently to all he has to say to them.

And now, may I venture to tell you, my children, that I wish you to go through a course of practical philosophy with me? It has always been my idea that woman's intellect is not sufficiently cultivated; that she is not sufficiently accustomed to reflect, to examine into questions, and to render an account of things to herself. Woman's mind on these points has always been treated with a disdain against which I have always felt bound to protest. Woman's intellect differs from man's; but if, in general, it has less breadth, large-mindedness, and connection of ideas, has it not also more delicacy of perception, more quickness of apprehension, and does she not often, by means of her feelings, succeed in thoroughly appreciating what a man only faintly perceives? It is my belief that were woman's understanding strengthened by a wise training, admirable results would be obtained, — results which would greatly astonish those who pretend that her proper sphere is the superintendence of the kitchen and other domestic matters. I explained my ideas on this head fully in the third discourse of the "Valiant Woman," and shall not now therefore recapitulate them. I merely wish to observe that in all the religious topics which we are about to discuss, I shall endeavor to point out to you the profound and beautiful harmony existing between religion and the heart and understanding of woman; and to explain how much truth, beauty, wisdom, and courtesy is to be found in the practices of Christian piety and in all the details of our worship. May it be granted me to excite in your souls a thirst for truth! For from the sources of truth flow fountains of the ever fresh and sparkling waters of life, with its depths of crystal clearness, which souls who have once tasted thereof neither can nor will forsake.

3

III.

Finally, my children, we shall learn to love and succor the poor. The poor are in one sense, and when their poverty is patiently borne, the special friends of our Saviour, and mercy to them, whatever may be their own merits or demerits, is one of the virtues most insisted on by the Gospel. I might even say that at the Day of Judgment one virtue only will be rewarded, that of charity to the poor; one vice only punished, hard-heartedness to the poor. For on that last day our Divine Saviour will say to His elect — "Come, ye blessed of my Father. For I was poor, and you gave Me to eat; I was sick, and you visited Me; a stranger, and you took Me in." Then, turning towards the wicked, He will exclaim — "Depart from Me, ye cursed, into everlasting fire. For I was poor, and you gave Me not to eat; I was sick, and you did not visit Me; a stranger, and you took Me not in." The just, astonished, shall say to God — "Lord, when did we see Thee in want?" And Christ will answer — "Amen, I say unto you, as long as you did it to one of these, my least brethren, you did it to Me." I am merely alluding now to these great truths, for I may perhaps find an opportunity of recurring to them a little later on.

Behold here, in one word, the great recommendation of our Association! It obliges you in a special manner to love and succor the poor. Now in order to love the poor, you must not take into consideration their dispositions, their good or bad qualities, their mental or bodily defects, for it is evident that from such a point of view the poor would not always present an attractive aspect. In order to love them, you must transfigure them until you can discern with the eyes of faith, hidden behind these moral and physical rags, Jesus Christ Himself, Who beholds us and solicits our aid. Under the Old Law, our Lord sometimes made Himself manifest in the form of angels' clothed with the figure of men; under the law of grace, and since poverty has been glorified at Nazareth and on Calvary, Jesus Christ often shows Himself under the garb of the poor. That is now His chosen raiment; and although the poor man himself may be unworthy of compassion, yet he who has pity on him in the name of Christ, loves and succors Christ Himself in his person. See here the only true source of love for the poor! You will find it in the Heart of Jesus, and it is there you must go to seek it. I do not mean to imply that alms should be given to all persons without inquiry, for, on the contrary, I hold that such indiscriminate charity leads to very mischievous results; but this is not the moment for entering into that question, I shall return to it at another time.

I wish you, my children, not only to love and assist the poor, but also and above all to visit them. "I was sick and poor," says Jesus Christ, "and you visited Me." Visiting the poor has inestimable advantages; it is a work most acceptable to God, and most meritorious to yourselves; which, when rightly understood and practised, becomes a source of the purest and truest happiness. Think of being able to say to yourself as you ascend some poor man's stair — It is

my Saviour Whom I am about to visit here; it is He
Who has sent for me, and Who will one day reward
with a crown of glory the steps I am now taking.
This is no pious fable. They are the words of our
Lord Himself — "Amen, I say unto you, when you
visit the poor and the sick, it is to Me that you do it."
Think of being able to say to yourself — A few moments more, and when I knock at the door of this
poor sufferer, our Lord Himself will say to me,
"Come in!" Such a thought may well make us
tremble; and yet it is true — true as the Gospel!

A lady of this Association once said to me —
"Whenever I feel more than usually unhappy, I go to
visit my poor people, and I always return consoled,
and even sometimes happy." Try this experience for
yourselves, my children, for it is a truth which human
nature cannot realize. God has placed the source of
the purest pleasures in the performance of apparently
mean and trivial good works, but faith is necessary in
order to understand and enjoy them; worldlings with
their false notions of happiness would probably compassionately smile at hearing such maxims enunciated.
And yet I am very sure that if weighed in the scales
of truth, it would be found that kind deeds and charitable visits to the poor have given more real enjoyment and more unmixed pleasure to Christian women,
than worldlings have ever derived from the crowded
balls and dazzling entertainments of fashion.

I would, then, recommend you to visit the poor as
much as is possible, and to have yourselves enrolled
on the list of the Visiting Ladies of this Association.
I am aware that this is not within the power of all,

and it is on that account that our Society has been divided into two categories. But let me beg of you to lay aside all pretexts for not putting down your names amongst the number of that holy militia, who are banded together in search of poverty and suffering, wherever they may be found. If you have really good reasons for not becoming one of the Visiting Ladies, I shall not insist further; but I must again caution you to beware that these reasons are not mere excuses. It may be that you are too fond of your ease, or it may be that you fear to inconvenience yourself, for there exists in some characters a certain indolence which leads to mental and bodily torpor. Shake off those chains; go visit the poor, and I hope before many months to hear you thank me for the counsel I am now giving you.

I have now, my children, freely laid before you my opinions and wishes. Let me be able to count with certainty on your zeal and devotedness under every trial. I am perhaps exacting a great deal, but I know that you can give a great deal, and that you are willing to do so. Your Archbishop desires to think of you as a society of Apostles, who, under his paternal direction, will help to extend the Kingdom of God; who will preach religion, not by sermons of words, but by the charm of their virtuous lives and the power of truth; who will draw together all classes of society by the softening influence of charity; and who will serve as a bond of union between rich and poor, and prepare the coming of the Kingdom of God, even in this world.

For me, my children, my chief recompense here

3*

below will be in doing you some little good, and assisting, through you, in lightening the poor man's lot. I shall rejoice in your triumphant vindication of the truths of the Gospel, and my hand shall be ever raised aloft to bless you — you and all dear to you. "The father's blessing establisheth the houses of the children." [1]

[1] Ecclus. iii. 11.

SECOND DISCOURSE.

SINS OF THE TONGUE.

"From the same mouth proceedeth blessing and cursing."—ST. JAMES iii. 10.

THE Apostle St. James sketches with a forcible hand and a powerful pen, the good and bad effects of the tongue. His words present a stern but true picture, and contain at the same time a programme of peace and concord for families and for society. " My brethren, in many things we all offend. If any man offend not in word, the same is a perfect man. He is able also with a bridle to turn about the whole body. For we put bits into the mouths of horses that they may obey us, and we turn about their whole body. Behold also ships, whereas they are great, and are driven by strong winds, yet are they turned about with a small helm, whithersoever the force of the gov-ernor willeth. Even so, the tongue is indeed a little member, and boasteth great things. Behold, how small a fire what a great wood it kindleth ; and the tongue is a fire, a world of iniquity. The tongue is placed among our members, which defileth the whole body, and setteth on fire the whole of our nativity, being set on fire by hell. For every kind of beast, and of bird, and of serpent, and the rest, is tamed, and hath been tamed by mankind : but the tongue no man can tame; a restless evil, full of deadly poison. By it we bless God and the Father ; and by it we curse men, who are made after the likeness of God. Out of the same mouth proceedeth blessing and cursing. My brethren, these things ought not so to be. Doth a fountain send forth through the same passage sweet and bitter waters ? . . . Who is a wise man, and en-dued with knowledge among you ? Let him show, by a good conversation, his work in the meekness of wisdom. But if you have bitter zeal, and there be contentions in your hearts, glory not, and be not liars against the truth. For this is not wisdom descend-ing from above, but earthly, sensual, diabolical. For where envying and contention is, there is inconstancy and every evil work. But the wisdom, which is from above, first indeed is chaste, then peaceable, modest, easy to be persuaded, consenting to the good, full of mercy and good fruits, without judging, without dis-simulation. And the fruit of justice is sown in peace to them that make peace." [1]

I propose, my children, to give you some instruc-tion on the tongue, and the faults which it causes us to commit; and I shall commence to-day by speaking of the power and the beauty of that organ, of the noble use which ought to be made of it, and of the many advantages which we may derive from it.

Speech is one of the sublimest things in this world, for it is the image of the Word of God. "Our speech

[1] St. James iii.

is the image of the Word, Who is the Son of God," [1] says St. Athanasius. There exists an eternal, infinite Word, in which God reflects back on Himself, as it were, the splendor of His Divine Being; and from this begotten Light proceeds Infinite Love, as It also proceeds from Him Who is the Fountain of the Divinity. This is the Word which the Father cast into the abyss of chaos, and with which He reproduced in the external world an incomplete image of the beauty of His Eternal Essence, — for the creation is but an image, an expression, a manifestation of God; it is the Word partly and visibly revealed to us. In like manner, man possesses the faculty of thought, the speech of the mind which he exercises in the sanctuary of his own soul, where he ponders over his ideas, meditates on the beauty of the exterior world; and then suddenly bursts forth by an act which we may compare to that of the Eternal Deity at the moment of creation; he speaks, that is to say, he displays to outward view what was before hidden in the depths of his own being; and should his ideas be lofty, sublime, and overflowing with good feeling and generous sentiments, his words pour themselves forth full of light and life; like a beam of sunlight, in which the most soft, delicate, and brilliant shades succeed each other with dazzling variety. By means of speech he can rouse an entire audience to enthusiasm, send forth an army on the road to victory, and promulgate laws which become the guide and the strength of a nation. This power of speech partakes of the elevated source whence it is derived, and it produces these

[1] Orat. ii. cont. Arian, n. 78.

marvellous and astounding effects because it has come from Heaven. "All the great and glorious things which speech has wrought," says St. Gregory Nyssa, "are a remembrance and an image of the Word of God." [1] Why are reasoning beings alone endowed with the faculty of speech? Because in God reason and speech are expressed by the same word, and the same creating act which raised us to the rank of intelligent beings, endowed us also with the gift of speech, while inarticulate sounds only were united to the instinct of brutes, sufficient to express their material wants, but inadequate to render intellectual ideas, which they do not possess. Man alone has the power of speech, because man alone is an intelligent being, and speech is a gift indispensable for him, in order that he may communicate his ideas to others.

The gifts of God are freely given; that is to say, that when Providence grants favors to men, it does not let itself be deterred by the foreknowledge of their abuse, nor does God withhold them because of the excesses to which that abuse sometimes leads. Man abuses everything, — genius, intellect, strength, and beauty. And yet God continues to endow human nature with genius, intellect, strength, and beauty; and all these great qualities are not the less reflections of God's perfections, and do not the less retain their union with the divine attributes amidst all these excesses. For example, speech is the gift of God which has been most profaned; man has made use of it to propagate errors, falsehood, and iniquity. These abuses cannot destroy the grandeur of its origin, nor

----

[1] De eo quid sit. Vol. ii. p. 34, edit. fol.

take from the innate beauty which must ever accompany it, even in its most lamentable misapplications.

You have all, my children, some time or other been present at some of those displays of fireworks which are so beautifully designed and splendidly carried out. How brilliant and all-pervading the light they throw around! How soft the reflected radiance of the colors! What an ever-varying succession of delicate tints and dazzling meteors! How the eye loves to bathe in those luminous waves of light! To revel in those swift, upward-flashing gleams, which burst and fall to earth again in sparkling, many-tinted cascades of color! This lovely spectacle elevates the mind, and calls up visions of another radiance more glorious and more entrancing far — the Spiritual and Infinite Light. Have you not also sometimes had an opportunity of still greater enjoyment, in listening to a flow of eloquent words? Beholding the light which streams from a great intellect and purified soul, and which sparkles on with many sweet, harmonious cadences, unveiling hidden treasures of which you had never had any idea, and opening up horizons hitherto unknown, thereby enabling you to participate in the grandest spectacle man can witness here below — the vision of the True and Beautiful, clad in forms divine. The same effect may be also produced in us by the perusal of a good book, writing being but another form of speech — thought translated in another manner, and made visible to our senses by a sort of natural incarnation.

" The flute and the psaltery make a sweet melody ;

but a pleasant tongue is above them both." [1]   If man
could not make known his thoughts, his feelings, and
his desires to others, life would resemble the Great
Desert, where nothing is heard but the sound of the
parching simoom, and the roar of the rising storm
raging on the far horizon.   Life, without means of
intercourse with kindred souls, — life thus completely
isolated, — would be but an anticipated death, a moral
and intellectual grave.   But speech is the light cast
by one intellect on another.   It establishes a current
of life between minds formed to comprehend each
other.   It is an echo which repeats itself throughout the realm of thinking beings; it causes springs
of living water to gush forth, and improvises charming oases in the desert of our existence, which would
otherwise be so sterile and monotonous.   Far from
being opposed to this intercourse, from which we draw
some of the most sensible sweetnesses and most god-
like pleasures of life, Christian piety authorizes and
encourages it; for it sees therein a means of develop-
ing the mind, perfecting its education, propagating
Christian ideas, and strewing flowers over the garden
of this life, which, without it, would be as desolate as
the scorched prairie.   "The words of the mouth of a
wise man are grace." [2]   "A wise man shall advance
himself with his words." [3]   "The heart of the wise
shall instruct his mouth, and shall add grace to his
lips.   Well-ordered words are as a honeycomb, sweet
to the soul and health to the bones." [4]   In another
place the Holy Spirit makes so much account of

[1] Ecclus. xi. 21.
[2] Eccles. x. 12.
[3] Ecclus. xx. 29.
[4] Prov. xvi. 23, 24.

speech, that He does not fear to say that "a good word is better than the gift." [1]

You must acknowledge that religion, rightly understood, lends a great charm and much happiness to our mortal life. Piety infuses seriousness into our existence, and seriousness is a requisite in every rational being; but piety also wishes us to possess, in union with gravity, kindliness, benignity, and all those characteristics of attractive virtue which are among its attributes as pointed out by the Wise Man. "For praise shall be with the wisdom of God, and shall abound in a faithful mouth." [2] "A wise man shall advance himself with his words." [3] Piety knows how grievously speech may be abused, but it also knows all its beauty and harmony and its many precious privileges.   I shall go on to indicate them briefly to you.

One of the ancients said that kind words partook of the nature of sweet perfumes.   They alleviate pain if we are suffering; they give us pleasure if we are in good health. [4] Such is the magic of kind words.   If you are suffering, if your heart is sore, if your inmost feelings have been cruelly wounded, go seek a faithful and trusty friend, lay bare before him those hidden, bleeding wounds which shrink from the public gaze; he will let fall on them the balm of a loving heart, and they will be healed by that divine elixir. [5] . You must gather up every drop of that pre-

---

[1] Ecclus. xviii. 16.   [2] Ecclus. xv. 10.   [3] Ecclus. xx. 29.
[4] Demophilus, Frag. Phil. Græc. p. 488, edit. Didot.
[5] "The tongue of the wise is health." — Prov. xii. 18. "A peaceable tongue is a tree of life." — Prov. xv. 4.

4

cious balm, and let it penetrate into every fibre; you must draw together the edges of that gaping wound, and on your return home you will experience a sensible amelioration. Thus are verified these words of Holy Writ — " A faithful friend is the medicine of life and immortality." [1] If, on the other hand, your soul be full of vigor; if your intellect be keen and abounding in thoughts and ideas; [2] and if your heart be throbbing with its own rich life of feeling; then are the loving words and the cheerful conversation of a devoted friend like the fresh and perfumed air of morning, which enhances the charms and doubles the pleasures of life. " Ointment and perfumes rejoice the heart, and the good counsels of a friend are sweet to the soul." [3]

In another place it is said that a good word — a word spoken in season — is like the kiss of peace given by one soul to another. " He shall kiss the lips that answereth right words." [4] In those words which come direct from the heart, full of warmth and earnestness, there is indeed all the outpouring of one mind into another, irradiating it with an electric flash from its own being. We have met with souls who have been converted by a single word; with souls whom that single word has brought back to the path of right, and kept therein. It was because that word bore the impress of a powerful mind, and carried with it a fund of light and heat. Such a word, especially when it is poured forth from the heart of a saint, has some-

---

[1] Ecclus. vi. 16.

[2] " The thoughts of the industrious always bring forth abundance." — Prov. xxi. 5.   [3] Prov. xxvii. 9.   [4] Prov. xxiv. 26.

thing of the wonder-working power and energy of the Divine Word — that Almighty Word which drew life out of nothing, and cast the seeds of good into the abyss of chaos.

The philosopher whom I quoted just now adds, that when a wise man speaks, it is as though a temple were opened, and the treasures of his mind rose up and unveiled themselves like so many statues. I remember having sometimes had the happiness of conversing with such men, whose minds resembled temples wherein great truths unfolded themselves like grand and beautiful pieces of sculpture. I experienced, in listening to them, a feeling of veneration mingled with astonishment and curiosity. As they spoke, I seemed to see fresh statues rise up before me, full of grace and dignity. I compared them one with another; each had been sculptured by a practised chisel, wielded by a skilful hand; each one was perfect of its kind, and the whole resembled one of those collections of *chefs-d'œuvre* where the workmanship is excellent in every detail. The conversation ended, I recalled to mind the words of the philosopher, that when the wise man speaks, his soul discloses itself like the interior of a temple. I carried away, imprinted on the tablets of my memory, a number of beautiful and admirable forms of human thought. Now, is not this also a Christian idea? Is not man's heart the temple of God? And when a just soul unveils its interior by means of speech; when the soul of a saint allows you to penetrate with the light of words of power into its inmost hidden sanctuary, how beautiful and affecting is the spectacle that you behold there! How splendid a collection of golden statues, symbols of all the virtues! How dazzling that crown of mysterious lamps, emblems of hidden truths — of those sublime truths of which the world is not worthy, but which God reveals to men of good-will.

St. Bonaventure, commenting on a sentence in Holy Scripture, says that the words of the wise are spurs to excite, or golden nails to retain.[1] And truly, a good word has often urged us forward in the path of right. How often has it been to us what the spur is to the horse! Look at that young courser. Is it growing tired, or does the sight of that steep bank affright it? It trembles, refuses, and cannot make up its mind to take the jump. The rider touches it with the spur, and, with a bound, it clears the fence, and rapidly pursues its course. Your soul had, perhaps, already begun to falter in the path of right; it was not advancing; it had, perhaps, even taken a step backwards. In such a moment you enter a church, where some striking idea falls from the preacher; or you hold a conversation with some grave and holy person, and from their lips you hear a thought that makes you ponder. That word, that idea, is the spur to rouse you from your apathy. Your soul shakes off its slumbers and takes courage; it walks firmly on, and makes rapid strides in the path of perfection, until at length virtue reigns forever triumphant in your heart.

And good words may also sometimes be likened to golden nails, to those holdfasts from which we hang

[1] In Lib. Sap. vi. vol. v. p. 846.

some precious object. "The words of the wise are as goads, and as nails deeply fastened in."[1] How often do we meet characters with excellent natural dispositions, but fickle, inconstant, and at the mercy of every wind! Their ideas are like nothing so much as leaves blown about by the wind in every direction; their feelings and resolutions are as running water, which is always changing its place, and ever rushing downwards without ceasing. One thing has been wanting to give steadfastness to their moral being: they have not had the benefit of those good counsels which would have been so many fixed points to secure their attention and serve as the immovable centre of their lives. They have never known those maxims which regulate life; those principles of transcendent wisdom which are the compass for the night of this world; they have never lived under the guidance of those experienced minds whose prudence gives an equilibrium to life; whose words and advice would have been for them golden nails whereon to hang the thoughts of the present and the plans of the future, thus elevating them to a safe height above human waves. "The words of the wise are as goads, and as nails deeply fastened in."

I will conclude this discourse, my children, by a sentence from the Wise Man — "Counsel in the heart of a man is like deep water, but a wise man will draw it out."[2] The best, the holiest, and the most enlightened men resemble deep wells, for they do not lightly bring their treasures to the surface like those volatile, superficial characters who talk much, have wise say-

[1] Eccles. xii. 11.
4*

[2] Prov. xx. 5.

ings always on their lips, but who apply them with an extraordinary want of intelligence, and even sometimes of good sense. You should, then, be able to distinguish between them and those men whose speech savors of truth, simplicity, and depth; but you will generally have to seek them in the shade, as you look for the nests of the sweetest songsters, who hide themselves in leafy shrubs and do not perch on the topmost boughs in order to be seen by every one. Volatile minds are too prone to go in quest of those everlasting talkers, those chattering birds, whose cry is loud, but who are wanting in discretion and devoid of all practical good sense: they find what they deserve to find. But serious minds worthy of knowing the truth will have the tact to discern the well-informed and the prudent, who can show them the light of Heaven and pour out for them the waters of wisdom. They will discover them principally by the calm of their minds, and their noiseless, tranquil habits, which are like to silent waters flowing from a deep spring. "Counsel in the heart of a man is like deep water, but a wise man will draw it out."[1] Counsel will, then, take its seat beside that Divine Will, and by the aid of manifold questions, of earnest interrogations, of searching and of digging deeply, will cause the waters to be poured forth in still greater abundance. The fountain was lying unused in the mind of the wise man, and now it has been changed into a torrent which overflows its banks. "Words from the mouth of a wise man are as deep water; and the fountain of wisdom as an overflowing stream."[2]

[1] Prov. xx. 5.   [2] Prov. xviii. 4.

THIRD DISCOURSE.

SINS OF THE TONGUE.

CONTINUED.

"But the things which proceed out of the mouth come forth from the heart." — ST. MATT. xv. 18.

ONE of the ancients was once asked, What is the tongue? "All that is best and all that is worst,"[1] he replied. The Holy Scriptures seem to allude to this truth, when they say — "Death and life are in the power of the tongue."[2] And assuredly the tongue is the noblest faculty man possesses; through its means he holds communion with his fellow-creatures, and maintains with them all those relations which are both a necessity and the charm of life. It is by means of the tongue, that key of the mind and heart, that the soul reveals its thoughts and feelings, and gives forth those tones so full of melody, power, and sweetness, that radiate around her, and make her a centre of attraction for other minds. "The flute and psaltery make a sweet melody, but a sweet tongue

[1] Anacharsis and Bias, quoted by Cornelius à Lapide, in Prov. xvii. 27, p. 476.
[2] Prov. xviii. 21.

is above them both." [1] All noble thoughts, liberal, high-minded ideas, holy and salutary inspirations proceed from the heart; but it is by means of words, whether written or spoken, that men come to an understanding with their fellow-men, and diffuse enlightenment and the fiery ardor of zeal around them. Happy the man whose intellect is keen, whose heart is on fire with a heavenly flame, and whose tongue is an instrument full of true and sweet accords. To him shall these words of Scripture be applied — " The mouth of the just is a vein of life. . . . In the lips of the wise is wisdom found. . . . They shall disperse knowledge." [2]

But, alas, why must there be a reverse to every medal? [3] The tongue is also the most active instrument for propagating sin and falsehood. With some people it is the channel through which all the foulness of the heart pours itself forth ; the interpreter through whom all earthly passions speak — such as pride, hate, wounded jealousy, revenge, and impurity ; or it is the quivering leaf perpetually agitated by the breath of a changeable, inconstant, and vainglorious wind. The tongue — " It is indeed a little member," as the Apostle says, "and yet it boasteth great things." [4] It is but a spark, but that spark can set fire to families and cities.

In our last instruction we spoke of the dignity and

---

[1] Ecclus. xl. 21.　　　　　　　[2] Prov. x. 11, 13; xv. 7.

[3] "A wicked word shall change the heart, out of which four manner of things arise, good and evil, life and death ; and the tongue is continually the ruler of them." — Ecclus. xxxvii. 21.

[4] St. James iii. 5.

divine origin of speech, and the marvellous effects which it has produced, and the two following shall be devoted to examining into the chief causes and the evil results of sins of the tongue.

" In the multitude of words there shall not want sin," [1] says the Holy Ghost.

The sins of the tongue; they are innumerable, and often a source of the very worst evils. The sins of the tongue; they are swallowed down like water, and strange to say, even in religious circles, people allow their tongues the same license on this head that worldlings do in theirs; and it is not a rare thing to meet with persons who believe themselves to be near perfection, yet who, after tearing to pieces their neighbor's reputation, will "piously wipe their mouths and say, I have done no evil." [2] Such persons do not see that they are grossly deceiving themselves, and that they shall receive a double punishment from the Lord. "And with a double destruction shall He destroy them." [3] "The tongue," says a pious author of the Middle Ages, "is as slippery as an eel and as sharp as an arrow; it alienates friends and multiplies enemies; it excites quarrels and sows discord; with a single stab it wounds and kills many at the same time; it flatters and deceives; it is to be found everywhere, always ready to withdraw good and replace it by evil." [4]

" Sins of the tongue," says St. Basil, "are the most familiar to our human nature, and are of many different kinds." [5] We will examine some of the principal

---

[1] Prov. x. 19.   [2] Prov. xxx. 20.   [3] Jer. xvii. 18.
[4] De interior Dom. cap. xxvii. inter opera Bern. 1. v. p. 537.
[5] In Psalm xxxiii. 1. i. p. 374.

ones, and you must permit me to speak to you with
my accustomed frankness.

At the bottom of your hearts is hidden a secret
pride which urges you to speak continually of yourself
and of your own merits, real, supposed, or exaggerated ;
for finding that others do not talk enough about you,
you have taken the resolution of avenging yourselves
by becoming your own advocates and pleading your
own cause with an ingenuity which, if not very re-
markable in itself, excites, at all events, much remark
from others.   Thence flow utterances as opposed to
truth as to humility, boastful narratives, clumsy, half-
veiled insinuations ; a tendency to lower and defame
others ; words wounding to those around you, and at
the same time injurious to truth, modesty, and the pre-
cepts of religion. When you cannot openly praise yourselves, lest your self-love should display itself in too
bold relief, and be too plainly visible even to the least
clear-sighted observers, you contrive by some skilful
manœuvre to succeed in extorting praise from others,
sometimes even from those actually present.   Your
wiles are plainly seen through, but from civility and
a wish to avoid giving offence, some silly and flattering compliments are improvised without a thought
whether they be true or not, and after you have
left, there will be a hearty laugh at the air of profound conviction with which you received the incense.
Such is the way of the world ; and therefore some
philosopher, I do not remember who, said that one
half the world was occupied in ridiculing the other
half.

Now listen to the counsels of religion.   True piety

will lead you to meditate often on your own misery and weakness, and without causing sadness or discouragement, it will teach you to have a thorough distrust of yourself; to know your own defects; to take every means of correcting them; to consult serious and experienced men; and to consult them in such a manner as to show them that you are sincere in your desire to be told the truth. After some months, perhaps some years, of this constant watchfulness over yourself, you will have humbled your pride; and, though you may not have entirely rooted it out, it will be no longer visible, and each day will lessen the number of its numerous offshoots. Then your tongue will lose the habit of talking perpetually about your own concerns. You will neither talk of them yourself, nor draw others into talking about them. You will cease making yourself the centre of conversation; you will not go about throwing ridicule, disdain, and discredit on every person who does not happen to suit you, because, without knowing it, they cast you into the shade, and are an obstacle to your pretensions. Both grave and trivial attacks on our neighbor have very often no other source than wounded vanity, and that self-love which is ever seeking to raise itself on the ruins of everything which excites its envy. If you follow these counsels you will avoid numerous sins against charity, while, at the same time, your conduct will be in accordance with the dictates of prudence and practical wisdom. You will not render yourselves unbearable, like certain persons I have known, who had become, without perceiving it themselves, the scourge of all conversation, by so constantly interspersing it with oft-told tales of their own experiences, that people at last came to the conclusion that such a "feast of reason" was, to say the least, very insipid and monotonous. Therefore does the Holy Ghost, after having said that "in the multitude of words there shall not want sin," add, "but he that refraineth his lips is most wise;"[1] as if to show us that the gifts of prudence and knowledge of the world are the accompaniments of virtue.

Does this mean that we are never to speak of ourselves? No, for it is quite permissible to do so, if done with tact, sound sense, prudence, and due regard to good manners, time, and place. For example, it is allowable to do so when we require to ask advice, and have light thrown on some question or other; or when the heart, having met with a discreet and faithful friend, pours itself forth like the overflowing rivulet, finding in this effusion all the support, and light, and consolation which are so necessary for us in this life. Except in these, and other analogous circumstances, it is better to avoid conversations where egotism is the principal seasoning, and all those personal allusions which, even when true, are wounding to the delicate, susceptible ears of others, whose self-love, with its jealous pretensions, are ever on the alert, watching us and listening to us.

I will now proceed with this abridged sketch of the Sins of the Tongue. You are harassed by a secret disease called jealousy. Naturalists who have studied the passions declare (I leave the resolving of that point to you), that while men have some defects

---

[1] Prov. x. 19.

peculiar to themselves, women possess theirs also; and that among these jealousy should not be set down in the last place. You are, then, peculiarly liable to jealousy or envy; for these two vices, whose signification is so dissimilar, and whose shades of difference are so strongly marked, are often confounded together in the French language. Jealousy acts on your eyes as a telescope of colored glass would do, making you see everything according to the varying tints of that unhappy passion. Some certain persons are the objects you have specially in view. The remembrance of them torments you like a ghost, disturbing your slumbers, and their name spoken in your hearing arouses a legion of insects, which irritate you from head to foot. The very thought of these people puts you in a fever; your heart is full of them, but it is a plenitude of bitterness, and their name and character quickly rise from the heart to the lips — and then, I pity them! They will get but scant mercy from you. They have probably never done you any wrong; they are, perhaps, quite ignorant of your animosity towards them; they are innocence itself; but you are of a jealous disposition, and therein lies their whole crime. You are jealous, and these people are too brilliant to please you, for jealousy is far readier to forgive defects than good qualities. They enjoy a certain amount of consideration, and perhaps hold a high position in the esteem and affections of others, and this gives birth to a feeling of inferiority in you. And there is yet another aggravating circumstance — the praises which you hear lavished on these people are a veritable martyrdom for you, a turning you on the gridiron! However, one need not be uneasy about you, for you know well how to revenge yourself, and pay off these accumulated injuries. You know how to find opportunities of speaking of your neighbor's faults, and also how to make those opportunities when they do not present · themselves naturally. You know how to wound him with the keen, envenomed arrows of sarcastic wit. Alas for that poor neighbor! In what way did he offend you? And how is he still a subject of annoyance to you? Merely because his virtues and good qualities are superior to your own. You know how to wrap up your bitter pills in sugared *bonbons* — that is, in honeyed words — with insinuations all the more treacherous that they are veiled under affected scruples and mysterious hints. I do not mean to assert that your neighbor must be irreproachable in your eyes, for no one is faultless. But you are here in the presence of God; speak sincerely, is not jealousy the chief cause of your rancor against him? Is not that feeling, strong as hell in its intensity, the cancer which is inwardly devouring you? Is it not the motive which prompts you to scatter broadcast the venom of your stinging words? If you do not take care, it will become a serpent urging you on to the blackest deeds? Were I preaching specially on this subject, I would dwell on it more at length; but to-day I shall only say that jealousy is one of those moral maladies which God alone can cure, particularly when it has attained a certain height, and reached the chronic stage. You must bring your heart before the altar of God, and let the flame of

Divine Love consume it; you must let the sword of Divine Justice cut away all that should be trodden under foot. You must have the courage to say to God — "Thee, O my God, Thee only I desire, and with Thee all that Thou willest! Do Thou cut, burn, and destroy all that displeases Thee, provided only that the flame of my heart may ascend more brightly to Heaven!" When this is done, your heart and tongue will be pure and clean. There is a common rule of health which falls daily under the notice of physicians, and which may be symbolically applied to our moral nature. When the body is full of humors, the tongue is foul; and on the other hand, it becomes clean as the body is purified; and when this is effected, it is a proof that the interior organization is sound and healthy. In like manner, morally speaking, who are the possessors of venomous tongues, — tongues which, as the Prophet says, stab with the virulence of the serpent — "And the viper's tongue shall kill him" ?[1] They are those creatures in whose veins poison lurks, and who secrete a fund of malignity in their hearts. But where the heart is pure, gentle, benevolent, and loving, kind words and charitable interpretations quickly rise to the tongue; and this principle is a reciprocal one. When physicians visit a sick man, they ask to look at his tongue, and the appearance of that organ furnishes a sure indication of the state of the health. Ah, if we could thus prove, from a moral point of view, the sanitary state of the tongue, what an insight would it not afford us into the interior of souls! The color of the tongue, and

[1] Job xx. 16.

the style of the conversation, would be an indication
of the tone of the mind.

Hatred and revenge are other sources whence arise
sins of the tongue. Some characters are naturally
spiteful, or at all events morose. A mere nothing
irritates, offends, and excites suspicion in their minds.
You wound them without being in the least aware of
it, and, with the very best intentions, you only succeed
in putting them out of temper; and then come those
rancorous feelings which eat into everything, like the
rust on old iron, — those deep-seated animosities, those
inflexible, angry resolutions, those plans of revenge
against certain persons, and sometimes against the
entire human race. Woe to that neighbor who becomes the object of your animadversion when you are
in that frame of mind. Once the flood-gates which
restrained the waters are burst open, woe to the unfortunate being who finds himself borne away on the
current of your angry words, and exposed to the
sharp edges of that tongue which cuts as keenly as a
razor. He will come off sadly wounded, at all events
in the thoughts and desires of those who thus drag
their brethren through the angry flood of their bitter
words. The Prophet says that some tongues are
sharp as razors: "As a sharp razor thou hast wrought
deceit." [1] The expression is eminently just, for the
comparison faithfully represents the features of the
original. Some tongues are indeed sharp razors;
how they cut, and carve, and hack to pieces! The
Prophet elsewhere tells us that some men "have
whetted their tongues like a sword." [2] They have

---

[1] Psalm li. 4.   [2] Psalm lxiii. 4.

got their bow all ready, and arrows which they have
steeped in venom, wherewith in the dark they shoot
the innocent man who walks in the uprightness of his
heart.[1] And in another place he calls to his aid the
most impressive symbols, desiring to express his meaning with the utmost force and truth, and he says, "A
man that beareth false witness against his neighbor is
like a dart and a sword and a sharp arrow."[2] Their
"teeth are weapons and arrows, and their tongue a
sharp sword."[3] And again he says of some men
that "the poison of asps is under their lips;"[4] that
"they sharpen their tongues like the serpent,"[5] and
that, like unto that reptile, they glide into the shadow
and "bite in silence."[6]

I have been thus exact in quoting for you the sayings made use of in Holy Scriptures for the reproba-
tion of this odious yet unfortunately common vice;
and whoever is conversant with human nature will acknowledge that the picture is a faithful one, that it is
human nature, — the corrupted side of human nature,
taken in the fact.

Our compassion should be reserved, not for those
persons who are the objects of all this bad feeling,
for if they be virtuous and united to their God it
can do them no harm, but for those, on the contrary,
who allow themselves to indulge in such feelings of
hatred and to infuse it into others; for those who
cherish hatred and nourish plans of revenge. Minds
so constituted do exist; like certain reptiles, they ab-

1 Psalm x. 3; lxiii. 4, 5.
2 Prov. xxv. 18.
3 Psalm lvi. 5.
4 Psalm xiii. 3.
5 Psalm cxxxix. 4.
6 Eccles. x. 11.

5*

sorb all that is poisonous in the air, ruminate it inte-
riorly, and then shed it forth around them. They
thus turn their food into wormwood, their drink into
gall, and only succeed in poisoning their own lives.
Ah! if they did but know the happiness that lies in
forgiveness, the relief found in daily unburdening our
consciences, exposing all the wounds of our hearts,
and pressing out their bitter drops at the foot of the
Cross, in order to bathe them afterwards with the
blood of Jesus Christ, to still their throbbings with
the spirit of the Saviour and the meekness of the
Gospel. If they could but understand the holy violence which a soul can exercise over itself, the peace
which follows from it, and the calm it produces in
heart and mind. If they could but understand the
mysterious reaction of deep and earnest Christian
feeling over our evil nature, how quickly they would
rejoice in God, how quickly triumph over the remains
of their bad instincts! How suddenly that flow of
bitter, angry, hasty, and spiteful words would be
checked and changed into accents of a gentle, rich,
benevolent, and loving charity.

Consider also the state of that mind, not exactly
impure, but light and frivolous, whose thoughts dwell
caressingly on the brink of sin, and whose imagination is clouded more or less voluntarily with such im-
ages, and whose spirit loves to recreate itself, I will
not say in, but near poisonous marshes. Glance at
their tongue, and you will find traces, and very often
numerous evident proofs, of that tendency. I am
convinced, my children, that it is possible to speak of
everything chastely. When the intention is pure,

and when prudence requires it, everything may be said with a conscience as pure as that of the angels, as the rays of the sun penetrate everywhere, and, after shedding light on the most obscure and muddy places, reascend again pure as ever to their home on high. But then, again, everything may be spoken of in an improper manner; a bad, at all events a light-minded person, will find opportunities for making unseemly jokes on any subject. You know that in music it is the key which determines the notes; the same note holding the same position on the gamut yet alters name and tone according to the key. There is in like manner a key to the soul. The intention, the tone of the voice, that indescribable something which a man can throw into his words when he wishes, these are the keys of the heart, which determine the real meaning of words and conversations. It is the breath of the soul passing through it which renders the same word good, bad, or indifferent. Why not avoid certain delicate topics? Why so greedy of hearing every report, whether scandalous or not? There are undoubtedly many things which must be known, and when we live in the world we cannot remain strangers to what passes around us, so that on this head I willingly make all the allowances which common sense requires. But whence comes that ungoverned appetite for certain kinds of food? Why make a display of an affected sensuality on the score of disedifying news? Why should there be any necessity for speaking so often of certain things? Why that feverish desire of knowledge *apropos* of certain subjects? Alas! is it not to be feared that some hidden canker exists in the soul corresponding to that thirst for forbidden fruit?

It were easy for me, my children, to take every human passion in turn, and show how each may give rise to conversations condemnable alike by faith and reason. The tongue is often made the instrument of our evil passions, and, as our evil instincts are more numerous than our good ones, the relation which exists between much talking and many sins is easily understood. "In a multitude of words there shall not want sin." [1] I do not know why it should be so, but good things are always the rarest. Prudent and circumspect conversations are soon brought to an end; their topics are not of a sufficiently wide range, and we are soon bored by them. This truth is not much to the credit of human nature.

I shall conclude with an observation which has an important bearing on our practical life. Speech has great power for good as well as for evil. It adds to the force of the thing spoken of, marking it out clearly with sharply defined points, like the many-sided facets of a diamond. At other times it recalls what we hear in the vaulted caves of Syracuse. I have there seen the guide take out a pistol and pull the trigger. The shot is fired, and the waves of sound roll on, rising each moment in force and sonorousness, until at length it had swelled to a tenfold power. Then it bursts with a sudden peal like the sound of a thunder-clap. Thus too does thought act; it lies in the depths of the soul like latent powder, and when we set fire to it by our words, it peals forth, echoing all around

[1] Prov. x. 19.

us, until it returns to us again, charged, perhaps, with storms and tempests. Let us now take up again for a moment the thread of our former reflections. You are jealous of some one, and entertain a violent antipathy to her. Her shadow seems to accompany you, until you are tempted to turn and look round, to make sure that she is not actually following you, so deeply has that one idea taken root in your brain. She is your "Old Man of the Sea," as the common proverb runs, and those popular sayings often conceal profound truths. Do you know what you must do to get rid of this oppressive dream, this nightmare, to call it by its true name? Go and pray fervently for a quarter of an hour at the foot of God's holy altar; or, if that is not possible, go do so in the sanctuary of your own heart. Lay bare your whole soul before God, and bewail your misery. Cast down all your littlenesses, your plots, your rancor, and your jealousies, cast them all down before Him; consider well their hideousness, have the courage to acknowledge your guilt and confess your faults; then lift up your eyes, look upon the countenance of your Saviour, and you will be healed. But alas! the venom of the adder is in your heart, and you persist in scattering it abroad on every side, in order that you may wound your enemy. You want to pay a visit: you set off hurriedly, arrive at your friend's house, and scarcely give yourself time to sit down before the sluice is raised, — I ought rather say, the embankment is broken. You converse then for a couple of hours, your tongue never ceases, fire flashes from your eyes and lips, until the torrent of your words carries everything before it like a flood. You drag your unfortunate neighbor over all the sharp stones along the wayside; and when you are at last again silent, it is only from lassitude, and not from any motives of charity. What do you gain by this outpouring of angry words? I am not now speaking of charity; that is oftener and more grievously sinned against than you are perhaps aware of. I am speaking of yourself, of your own interests, of the interior calm of your own mind. You return home only more fatigued and more dejected after such conversations. It is true you have had the miserable satisfaction of tearing your neighbor's character to atoms; you have made a sort of mince-meat of it, and seasoned it with *sauce piquante;* but the greater portion of pepper, salt, and vinegar employed has been absorbed into your own character, and if you still retain any feelings of religion you must necessarily experience some remorse. What do you gain, I must ask you once more, by playing such a contemptible part? At first you felt a slight difficulty in breathing; now you are choking with rage, and that is all the reward you get. Even when looked at from the point of view of reason, silence must always be the best way of healing and of calming the wounds inflicted on the heart; exposing them to the public gaze only inflames them, while talking irritates and increases the suffering tenfold.

I make one exception, and one only, to this rule; and that is, — when the heart has need of light and counsel, support and consolation; when it is too full, and must unburden itself lest it should break; when the soul is thrown back on itself, and is vainly seeking, not reprisals, but a staff to keep it upright in its path, — then the heart is soothed, strengthened, enlightened, and supported by words of counsel; then the bosom of a devoted friend, into whom we can pour our troubles, becomes for us the breast of a mother, which soothes and lulls to sleep all the agonies of our souls. Far from prohibiting such outpourings, I earnestly desire them for you. May you be so fortunate as to meet hearts worthy of your confidence, and deserving it by their sincere affection, tried discretion, and true and steady friendship. But do not forget that you must be careful to avoid all exaggeration, for wounded hearts are prone to see more than there really is, and even sometimes to see what does not exist at all. Beware of framing your questions so that they can only be answered in the way you wish; nothing is more usual, more common, or more deceitful than such a practice. Be frank and open, and you will be able to verify in your practical life the truth of those words of Holy Writ — "Ointment and perfumes rejoice the heart, and the good counsels of a friend are sweet to the soul." [1]

Make the resolution, my children, of talking less, that you may live in peace and commit fewer sins. Say to God with the Prophet — "Who will set a guard before my mouth, and a sure seal upon my lips, that I fall not by them, and that my tongue destroy me not." [2] O Lord, my God, do Thou purify my lips, or rather my heart, for that is the source of all good. The heart is the fountain, the lips but the channel through which the waters flow, such as they come

---

[1] Prov. xxvii. 9.   [2] Ecclus. xxii. 33.

from the parent source. Grant, O my God, that springs of truth, goodness, and holiness may ever be found in my heart, and when I pour them forth, do Thou direct all that it contains to Thy greater glory and the good of my brethren.   Amen.

FOURTH DISCOURSE.

SINS OF THE TONGUE.

CONTINUED.

"There is one that holdeth his peace, because he knoweth not what to say: and there is another that holdeth his peace, knowing the proper time." — ECCLUS. xx. 6.

"And there is one that holdeth his peace, he is wise." — ECCLUS. xix. 28.

THE habit of talking much generally comes from our ill-governed passions, and it daily exposes us to the commission of a great number of faults. It is a passion which often makes us come out of ourselves, and shed the superabundance of our souls all about us; it is pride, which loves to take up a position, to put itself forward, and cleverly lead others to think and talk about ourselves. It is envy and jealousy, which cannot bear any good in others, which desire their own pleasure exclusively, which consider it both a duty and a right to decry everything which seems to lie in their path, and to brush away the bloom of esteem and love surrounding every rival. It is hatred and a spirit of revenge, which gather interior bile, and discharge it at stated intervals, as if it were the ap-

pointed means for unburdening the heart and com-
forting the soul. Or yet again, it is the frivolity of a
mind that pretends ignorance of the vocabulary of
unhealthy places, and yet savors with relish words
whose meaning is transparent enough, or expressions
of double meaning; which finds in very shady tints a
heartfelt satisfaction, and knows no fear in walking
along the very brink of a precipice.

These words are then very true, that "in the multitude of words there shall not want sin." The virtuous soul loves to converse with God rather than with
men; but passion, whatever form it assumes, has just
the contrary tendency, — it must give itself vent, although doing so increases its intensity. Speech is
a hammer, forcing down and riveting our feelings.
"He that hateth babbling extinguisheth evil,"[1] saith
the Holy Scripture, for it is as though the wind had
ceased, when the fire must needs go out.

I will examine in this discourse the inconveniences
resulting from sins of the tongue.

I.

"Empty vessels resound the loudest," says one of
the ancients; "and those who have least sense are the
greatest talkers."[2] Generally speaking, noise is in
inverse ratio to truth and genuineness, and solid
things are the least sonorous. The same law holds
good with all that shines too brightly; fixed stars are
less brilliant but more steady, while meteors, whose

---

[1] Ecclus. xix. 5.   [2] Ausonius.

light is dazzling, soon disappear, for they have no consistence. "Hast thou seen a man hasty to speak?" says the Scripture; "folly is rather to be looked for than his amendment."[1] The human mind has only a certain amount of prudence, intelligence, and good sense at its disposal; the treasure is limited with every one, and is reducible to a very small quantity in some. It evidently results from this, that if we persist in constantly showing off, making a perpetual exhibition of our intellectual possessions, our imaginary wealth of mind, we can only end by displaying our misery and poverty; and the interior, thus exposed to the public gaze, will sometimes resemble those wretchedly tenanted shallows which are laid bare to view when the tide is out. And the Scriptures say again, "Wise men lay up knowledge, but the mouth of fools is next to confusion."[2] And in another place, "A cautious man concealeth knowledge, but the heart of fools publisheth folly."[3] Modesty and reserve of speech are therefore proofs of merit. The man who feels himself possessor of a great treasure will not lavish it foolishly in public, but will keep it concealed, and distribute it only at the call of charity, and according to the dictates of prudence. But when speech, that vase which holds the treasures of thought, begins to ring loudly, it is a sign its contents are nearly exhausted.

See, my children, how everything in the domain of right principle meets and combines together. I think I have said before that what is true and genuine must necessarily be simple and an enemy of all noise.

[1] Prov. xxix. 20.   [2] Prov. x. 14.   [3] Prov. xii. 23.

Here again is an application of the maxim that great talkers are seldom people of sense. Holy Writ possesses on this subject, as on so many others, several proverbs, which are so many good coins struck from the purest gold, and whose only defect is being so little known. It says — "Where there are many words there is oftentimes want."[1] A sentence full of wisdom, which, if applied to the questions of life, would act like a powerful steam-hammer, demolishing at a blow all the false, showy appearances under which men hide their real selves. You see that person or that advertisement that is making such a noise in the world, drawing every eye and attracting every one's attention. Beware of them : if the splendor and the rumors exceed a certain point, be on your guard, and not in too great a hurry to pronounce any opinion. I do not mean that you are to judge and condemn before you know all the particulars, but that you should examine closely, and take your stand on the ground of reserving your opinion, and perhaps you will see the conclusion drawn by the Wise Man verified in whole or in part — "Where there are many words there is oftentimes want." Theocritus said, speaking of a great talker, that though his words were poured forth in a flood, there was not a drop of good sense to be found amongst them.[2]

In proportion as we advance in life, and that our intercourse with men and business adorns our brows with a crown of silver hairs, symbols of the grave teaching of experience, we find that we know less than we thought, we unlearn many things, and grow

[1] Prov. xiv. 23.   [2] Quoted by Corderius, in Job i. 32.

less positive about our own judgment. We feel the need of bowing our head in our hands and being silent, while every day takes from the list of our beliefs. Happily for us, God always remains enshrined in the depths of our soul, and our faith in the Divine increases as our earthly convictions fade. For this cause, you will always find in serious-minded men a tendency to be silent; to live in themselves; to ponder over the events of life without pronouncing judgment on them; to nourish a kind of instinctive distrust, of which silence is the expression. And from that, too, comes that caution and reserve of speech which sets off a high-toned mind, as delicate engraving enhances the beauty of a gem. The man who knows nothing believes that he is acquainted with everything; he never doubts or mistrusts himself, though his knowledge must be always superficial, as he judges from the narrow point of view of a frivolous mind. His conversation is consequently interminable, and his words an inundation, which bears a direct inverse proportion to the small amount of good sense they contain. "A fool multiplieth knowledge,"[1] and the Scripture also says, in a sentence as forcible and just as it is happily expressed — " The mouth of fools bubbleth out folly."[2] Once on a time, when Demosthenes was present at a feast, some one having spoken unceasingly and on every subject, the celebrated orator said to him at the end of the repast — " If you really knew so much, friend, you would talk less."[3] Might not this sensible remark be applied to many? If all that people said were dictated by good sense

[1] Eccles. x. 14.   [2] Prov. xv. 2.   [3] Stob. 37.

6*

and a well-instructed mind, at least one-half, perhaps
three-quarters, of the usual conversations we hear
would never be uttered.   Neither should we have any
cause for complaint in this, for justice, truth, prudence, and charity would be the gainers.   Has not
La Bruyere said, alluding to the ordinary conversations of the world — " If we really paid attention to
all the vain, puerile, and supercilious words uttered
in conversation, we would be ashamed either to say
them or to listen to them." [1]

Do not imagine, however, that I am recommending
a taciturn behavior to you.   Assuredly not; and I
even hope to show you, in my next discourse, that
charm of manner, courtesy, reserve, and good sense
agree perfectly together.   " The tongue of the wise
adorneth knowledge," [2] says the Holy Ghost.   It is
not heavy tropical rain which best refreshes a delicate
plant; but the gentle dew, which falls softly drop by
drop, and reposes tranquilly on its petals.   Neither
are precipitate opinions, nor a flood of words, any attraction in conversation; its charm consists in circumspect speech, where discretion is united to a win-
ning frankness.

I am far from recommending a gloomy silence to
you.   That would be only a scourge of another description, rendering all our social relations as cold and
dreary as the ice-bound winter.   I confine myself to
saying with the Holy Ghost — " The man of understanding is of a precious spirit." [3]   A comparison
borrowed from your own habits will, perhaps, make
my meaning clearer.   You often carry a bottle of

<hr>

[1] De la Société, ch. v.   [2] Prov. xv. 2.   [3] Prov. xvii. 27.

pungent salts about you, which, though useful and pleasantly perfumed, are also volatile, and quickly evaporate if exposed to the air. You may open the glass which contains them occasionally, but not too often, for they would thus lose all their pungency, and would revive you no more with their balmy essence.

La Rochefoucauld says, "Men speak little, unless when prompted by vanity. . . . As it is the mark of a great mind to say a great deal in a few words, so, on the other hand, a little mind has the faculty of speaking much, yet saying nothing." [1]

II.

Great talkers weary others and expose themselves to ridicule. One of the ancients was accustomed to say that "the best men were those who spoke least. . . . And that if chatterers only suffered as much themselves as they made others suffer, they would be quickly cured of their love of talking." [2] I once knew one of those incessant talkers, who was also intent on button-holing others. From early morn he sought to lay hold of some unhappy listener, and if he succeeded, kept him nailed to the post all day. He was as much dreaded as an inundation might have been, and the torrent of his eloquence was so continuous, that some subtle manœuvre was necessary in order to escape from him. You will tell me this is an extreme case, rarely to be met with. True; but

---

[1] Maxims, cxxxvii. cxlii. p. 160, edit. Didot.
[2] Apollonius. Stob. sec. 37.

alas! how many less strongly marked shades of this nature do we not meet, when passing from that extreme to the opposite quarter of agreeable and discreet persons? One of the plagues of society is meeting with these sponge-like natures, always ready to be filled and emptied, from whom the slightest pressure squeezes out all that is in them, until those who are in their neighborhood run the risk of being deluged. Woe to all who have to walk between these dripping eaves! They come out with wits half frozen and paralyzed. A douche of cold water would be far preferable, for reaction would quickly restore warmth and strength to their organization. Listen to what the Holy Ghost says — " The talking of a fool is like a burden in the way." [1] See that poor traveller toiling weariedly along, showing evident signs of fatigue; for the heat of the day, the roughness of the road, and the length of the journey have combined to exhaust him. Would you think to refresh and comfort him by placing a burden on his shoulders? Yet such, says the Holy Spirit, is the conduct of those incessant talkers; for they place the load of their interminable discourses on the shoulders of their poor fellow-creatures, who have already enough to do in bearing up under life's heavy burdens. The Holy Scriptures add — " As a house that is destroyed, so is wisdom to a fool," [2] thus likening the torrent of unconsidered words to a ruined house where stones lie about, encumbering the way and adding to the fatigue of both eyes and feet.

You must, then, practise these wise counsels, if

---

[1] Ecclus. xxi. 19.   [2] Ecclus. xxi. 21.

you wish neither to bore nor annoy the society you frequent. Seek to observe that moderation in speech which is both a proof of wisdom and a great charm in conversation. Do not try to monopolize all the talk to yourselves ; talk, but allow others to talk also, and if there must be any excess, let it be on the side of silence. Let your conversation resemble a feast, from which one stands up with unabated relish, not with the satiety of repletion. The Holy Ghost says — " In the lips of the wise grace shall be found, and the mouth of the prudent is sought after in the Church, and they will think upon his words in their hearts." [1]

An English politician gave this advice to his son — " Wear your learning, like your watch, in a private pocket, and do not pull it out and strike it, merely to show that you have one. If you are asked what o'clock it is, tell it ; but do not proclaim it hourly, and unasked, like a watchman." [2] There are very many persons who love to display their wit, as little children take pleasure in showing off their pinchbeck watches, and making them strike the hour. There is nothing more tiresome, after the wearisome length of some people's conversation, than that petty self-love which is always sounding its own praises, and giving the benefit of its own insignificant personality. It is the surest, the most infallible means of boring others and making ourselves ridiculous — " The mouth of the fool is next to confusion." [3]

[1] Ecclus. xxi. 19, 20.
[2] Chesterfield, Letter 110, vol. i. p. 215, edit. Charpentier.
[3] Prov. x. 14.

III.

" The tongue is a little member," says the Apostle;
"behold how small a fire, what a great wood it kindleth." [1] I am convinced, my children, that the
greater part of the misfortunes which weigh so heavily on individuals, families, and society generally have
their commencement in the imprudent or malicious
speeches of some bad tongue. Incendiarism in the
moral world usually springs from that fatal spark.
You see a divided household, a disunited family : what
is the cause of it all? Some unseen viper's tongue
stole amongst them, discharging its venom in secret.
And there again are friends estranged by the tongue
of a third person, whose thoughtless, false, and lying
words have divided their hearts. " The tongue of a
third person hath disquieted many." [2] " The beginning of quarrels is as when one telleth out water," [3]
says the Holy Ghost; and he who opens the flood-
gates of incautious and satirical observations can
never calculate the ravages he may cause in the field
of humanity. My limits will not now permit me to
speak on this subject as fully as its importance would
require. I should have to describe all the evils which
sins of the tongue occasion in society; explain the
strict obligation binding the culprits to repair the injuries they have done their neighbors by their intem-
perate language; and remind Christians that although
charity holds the first place among the virtues, according to our religion, it is the one most frequently
outraged by them. It was said of the early Chris-

[1] St. James iii. 5.   [2] Ecclus. xxviii. 16.   [3] Prov. xvii. 14.

tians, writes Cardinal de Cheverus, "Behold these Christians, how they love one another!" and nowadays it might be said, "Behold these Christians, how they hate one another!" But these reflections would carry me too far; and their right place is in a special treatise on charity, or rather, in one on slander or calumny. I shall therefore pass on to other inconveniences which may result from indiscretion in speaking. The Arabs have the following proverb — "As long as you remain silent, you are the master of your words, and the ruler of your thoughts; but once spoken aloud, those thoughts become your ruler."

You, too, my children, may have cause to regret some such speeches, which, despite yourselves, have influenced your whole lives, establishing a dominion over you, weighing down your heart, and filling it with long-enduring and poignant sorrow. You made some observation, perhaps most innocently, and without attaching any importance to it; but it was taken hold of by some perverted heart, some jealous, malignant mind, of which there are so many in this world! Those words raised a storm in your life, — a storm which, perchance, has lasted many years. You were, perhaps, imprudent, and said things which had better been left unsaid; but you were irritated, and in some moment of bitterness gave utterance to some unhappy remarks, which you did not really mean, but which escaped your lips because your heart was sorely wounded. Had they been spoken in the ear of a friend, they would have fallen therein, as into a deep well, and died without an echo. But, unfortunately for you, they have been intentionally kept in mind,

like a weapon suspended over another's head; and
after many years the blade is lifted up to pierce your
own heart, and fill your life with bitterness.[1]

You cannot keep too strict a guard over your
tongue, if you desire that your path in life should be
a peaceful one. The Holy Ghost testifies to this,
when he says — " He that keepeth his mouth keepeth
his soul; but he that hath no guard on his speech
shall meet with evils." [2] It is true that, no matter
what precautions you take, you cannot escape calumny, and evil tongues will seek to work you harm.
When you are silent, they will affirm that you spoke;
and when you have made some harmless remark, they
will give you credit for volumes of sly, perfidious
meaning. It is not possible to escape the slanders of
spiteful people in this world. Our Lord Himself, His
Apostles, and all His Saints, were not exempted from
this sad law of human life. This world is full of
those malevolent creatures, who seem to play here
below the part of venomous reptiles, — that is, they
seem to secrete their natural venom in order maliciously to inoculate their neighbors with it. How
much worse will it not then be if you have given occasion for their malice? If by some hasty, thoughtless words you have furnished subjects for the ever-
ready comments of jealousy, hatred, suspicion, and
calumny? Take heed, then, about what you say;
reflect much before you speak, particularly when any

---

[1] "And take heed lest thou slip with thy tongue, and fall in the
sight of thy enemies who lay in wait for thee, and thy fall be incurable
unto death." — Ecclus. xxviii. 30.

[2] Prov. xiii. 3.

important matters are under discussion; when your neighbor's character is at stake, and the circumstances are grave. A single word may precipitate your life down an abyss, to use an expression of Holy Writ — "The lips of a fool shall throw him down headlong." [1] Watch over yourself ˉwith the utmost care, that you may preserve your soul from anguish — "He that keepeth his mouth and his tongue keepeth his soul from distress." [2]

Watch all the more carefully because discreet listeners are so rare. Discretion is a pearl rarely met with; you will find excellent persons, well-intentioned, and devoted to you; but with all that, they are of that nature whose tissue is formed of some open-work netting, — everything passes through it, almost without their being conscious of it. Why do you choose them as the depositaries of a secret? You, not they, should be looked on as the culprit. Telling a secret to some characters is like hanging a weight round their necks, or throwing them into some stifling atmosphere beyond their powers of endurance, — they break into violent perspiration, and everything seems to exude from their pores. St. Ambrose says of such persons — "They are so full of issues, that everything confided to them escapes again; they are drunk with loquacity." [3] And the Holy Ghost says — "As a city that lieth open and is not compassed with walls, so is a man that cannot refrain his own spirit in speaking." [4]

---

[1] Eccles. x. 12.
[2] Prov. xxi. 23.
[3] In Psalm cxviii. Serm. iv. vol. ii. pp. 1246, 1247.
[4] Prov. xxv. 28.

" Hear, O ye children, the discipline of the mouth, and he that will keep it shall not perish by his lips, nor be brought to fall into most wicked words;"[1] receive it as a means of avoiding many miseries, disappointments, and misfortunes. There is an old proverb, which cannot be too often repeated, because, though every one approves of it in words, they commonly tread it under foot in practice — " You will often regret having spoken, never having kept silence." Remember that he who knows when to hold his tongue remains master of his thoughts, his words, and his own soul. On the other hand, a single word often becomes for us a key that we have ourselves given into the enemy's possession; a weapon that we have sharpened against ourselves; a tyrant whom we have placed in authority over us; a full charter, which gives a right to another over all our possessions, and reduces us to the most terrible, lasting, and irredeemable bondage.

Admire here how virtue, when laying down rules for our moral guidance, is to us a fountain of wisdom and real happiness. The counsels of the Holy Ghost, on Whose words I have simply commented, will be as a fence around your life, preserving it from the attacks and prying glances of the outer world. The Holy Spirit, when recommending discretion and reserve in speech to us, is implanting the seeds of peace and security in our lives. The philosophy of the ancients included this wise practice, for it tells us by the mouth of the Greek tragedian — " Learn to be silent, O my son, for silence is the source of much good."[2]

---

[1] Ecclus. xxiii. 7.　　　[2] Sophocles, Frag. p. 353, edit. Didot.

St. Nilus gives the following advice to a Christian — " Learn how to keep secrets ; construct massive gates wherewith to close the entrances into your mind, fasten them with trusty bolts, and place on them the seal of determined silence." [1] If we did not know human nature we might think these precautions excessive, for surely never were fastenings more complicated. But our daily experience teaches us that in such matters we cannot take too many precautions against thieves, of whom the one most skilful and most to be feared is he who resides within, — our own frail nature, joined to that fatal attraction which is ever leading us to talk of ourselves and others in a way that is compromising both to our consciences and our own interests. Let us then keep guard over our tongues, and our souls shall be free from anguish. " He that keepeth his mouth and his tongue keepeth his soul from distress." [2]

---

[1] Epist. clviii. bk. ii. p, 275, edit. Migne.   [2] Prov. xxi. 23.

FIFTH DISCOURSE.

SINS OF THE TONGUE.

CONTINUED.

"The heart of the wise shall instruct his mouth, and shall add grace
to his lips." — Prov. xvi, 23.

Man is born for companionship, and he feels within
himself a sweet but irresistible power, forcing him to
cast in his life with the common lot, to unite it with
that of others, to give to his brethren, and to receive
from them in his turn, the superabundant treasures
of heart and intellect. The tongue is one of the
principal organs marked out for transmitting them.
It is the bridge of communication, suspended between
two worlds, which loses itself on one side in the
invisible regions of the spiritual, and rests on the
other on the world of the senses, that it may reach
those minds which have taken up their position on
the opposite bank of the stream. The tongue, as
well as the eye, is a bright but mysteriously veiled
transparency, through which the soul suffers itself to
be seen, and reveals more or less clearly its heavenly
beauty.

But if the heart be corrupt, foolish, and a prey to

unbridled passions, the suspension bridge will be worn by the traces of every form of iniquity, by the hasty footsteps of pride, hatred, jealousy, and wounded self-love; and also by all the faults, follies, and imprudent acts of a heart that is not directed by prudence. After having thus pointed out the grandeur and the beauty of speech, the defects and excesses to which the tongue is prone, it remains for me to lay down some rules for your guidance in conversation.

I.

Prudence is the first quality needed. Prudence is man's guiding clew through the labyrinth of this world. It is virtue's charioteer, as the Saints termed it. Prudence is the pillar of light going before and teaching us, not only what we must do and say, but also the manner of speaking and acting. There are many things which may be unhesitatingly said before certain persons, when they may even be productive of the happiest results. But repeat them before others whose minds are warped and distorted (and their number is a very considerable one), or repeat them before some badly disposed hearts (and who can count these in the world?), and you may be sure that the words, however excellent they may be in themselves, will have a bad effect. They will be turned against you, and serve as a text for malignant commentaries. Have you ever remarked the singular effect produced by light, and the strange decomposition it undergoes when it passes through dark

7*

tinted colored glass, or through streaked panes, disfigured by unevenness and blotches? The pure light of heaven, so clear, so bright, so direct, so radiant in itself, seems to have entirely changed its nature. It becomes darkened and sombre, its rays are obscured, its pathway distorted, its lines crooked, — an image of what we see every day occur in conversation. Some pure, upright mind lets fall an observation as spotless as the sunlight, but it is laid hold of by some malicious person with a distorted mind and a perverted heart. That simple remark is given a bad turn, that pure thought stained, that straightforward idea distorted and forced into an oblique direction. There results from all this some strange medley, not having the slightest resemblance to the original idea, but which is put before the public as the real meaning of the words. Joubert said — "Project strong lights on a naturally dense mind and you will see to what a degree it will obscure them." [1] I too would say, in an analogous sense, lay noble ideas, high-minded principles, and important considerations before narrow, prejudiced minds and badly disposed hearts, and you will see to what a point everything will be perverted.

Watch, then, with the utmost care not only over your words, but also over the vessels into which you pour them, and the minds with which you hold communication. Seek to acquire sufficient discernment of character to enable you to distinguish the capacity of each one and the amount which he can bear. You do wrong to pour a strong generous wine into a slight

---

[1] Pensées, tit. iv. vol. i. p. 171. Second edition.

flask, for the glass is thin, and it may burst and fly, and you yourself suffer from the fracture. Putting this counsel into practice is one of the things most difficult to be done in this life, because nothing can be more difficult than thoroughly to know the human mind in all its wonderful variety — the capabilities of each person, what he can bear, what may produce happy results or bring about deplorable consequences; but the difficulty experienced in a work can never diminish its necessity. A Greek philosopher says — " The musician tunes his lyre, and the wise man brings his mind into harmony with other minds." [1] I will add that the best way of keeping ones self in unison with a certain order of minds is to be silent on many topics. When we have ascertained the prejudices which the slightest touch converts into sharp points, we avoid them; when we have found blossoms behind which lurk thorns to prick the fingers of those who gather them, we refuse to pick them, and wait for a better opportunity with minds of another calibre. Silence is often the only means of preserving peace and concord.

" Prudence," as St. Bonaventure remarks, " points out to us what we ought to say, to whom we ought to say it, how strongly, and in what measure we ought to express it." [2] And if we neglect those circumstances of time, manner, place, and character, though we may speak the truth, we are yet not doing it in a right manner.[3] Fénelon divides all persons with whom we have communication into three classes: men in

---

[1] Demophilus.   [2] Pharet. bk. iv. ch. xxxiv. vol. vii. p. 408.
[3] In Hexæ. Serm. ii. vol. viii. p. 36.

general, our acquaintances, and our intimate friends. With the first we must cultivate a spirit of charity and fidelity to our duties; with the second the opening is wider, although it does not yet reach to the borders of intimacy; but with the third our confidence should be unreserved, — "only," as the Archbishop of Cambray says, "such persons are rarely to be found." [1]   I hold that this classification admits of subdivisions, whose shades of difference are distinct, although difficult to define.

Let us reflect a little on a counsel to which the Scriptures frequently revert, that of speaking at the right time. "To speak a word in due time is like apples of gold on beds of silver." [2]   "A parable coming out of a fool's mouth shall be rejected, for he doth not speak it in due season." [3]   "A tale out of time is like music in mourning." [4]   Besides this, it is a maxim of universal wisdom, and applicable to everything — to our actions, words, and silence. The Holy Ghost says, "There is a time and opportunity for every business." [5]   Some characters have the unhappy knack of doing and saying everything at the wrong time; they give a crooked turn to everything good, and have a way of putting in such an odd setting, and expressing in such an awkward fashion, the most undisputed maxims of wisdom, that these very maxims and teachings become utter folly in their mouths. And it is because of this that St. Bonaventure says, "That we find fault with the counsels of prudence on the lips of a foolish man, because he

[1] Lettres Spirit. bk. viii. vol. xciii. p. 525, edit. Leroux.　[2] Prov. xxv. 11.
[3] Ecclus. xx. 22.　　　　[4] Ecclus. xxii. 6.　　　　[5] Eccles. viii. 6.

does not know how to speak them at the right moment."[1]

Alas for the weakness of the human heart! Alas for the inconstancy of our feelings and sentiments! It seems as though a word, good and true in itself, ought always to produce good effects. And yet, such is the fickleness of our thoughts and desires, and such also the constant changes in the events of life, that despite ourselves, and through an involuntary chain of causes and effects, that which was good yesterday becomes evil to-day. The variation induced by the many accidents of life calls for other remedies, that is, other words and different advice, for good counsels are often the best and only remedy of the soul. We must, then, endeavor to ascertain, by prudence and kindliness, the real qualities of the ground wherein we deposit the seed of our souls. This is assuredly a difficult thing to do, for who can fathom the abysses of the human heart, and all its contrary currents? "Where there is no hearing pour not out words,"[2] says the Holy Ghost. What marvellous tact is requisite to find the right clew to this labyrinth; perfectly to discern time, quantity, quality, and character, with the alterations hourly wrought by the many modifications of life? Nevertheless, it is the right appreciation of all these different shades which constitutes what one of the Fathers of the Church called "the varied science of conversation, the diversified power of speech."[3]

---

[1] Specul. ad Novit. vol. i. ch. xx. bk. xiii. p. 45.   [2] Ecclus. xxxii. 6.

[3] "He who has this varied power of speech, in due season aptly furnishes to each one of his hearers what is of use to him." — St. Greg. Nyss. Serm. ix. on the Cant. vol. i. p. 959.

II.

The second counsel which I shall give you is to
mingle a little seriousness with your topics of conversation. La Bruyere thus defines a worldly life: "To be
incessantly seeking each other, impatient at not meeting, yet meeting only to talk about trifles."[1] Yet,
my children, trifles, splendid nothings, disguised under high-sounding words and affected protestations!
— is not this the way of the world? And ought we
not, even looking at it from a Christian point of view,
to esteem ourselves fortunate when trifles only form
the staple of conversation? About what do men talk
in the world? I am not now alluding to dangerous
and sinful conversations, nor to such as are grievously wounding to charity. What are the usual topics? Dress, parties, balls, rumors of every kind.
Such a one was at that person's ball; and her toilet
from head to foot, her looks and her words, are all
criticised. Two others were seen to meet in the
street, when a rather extraordinary scene was en-
acted at such a place of the pavement. What more
shall I say, my children, to describe a conversation
ever of the world, worldly; gathering up all the waifs
and strays of fashionable *salons*, and picking up every
stray leaf blown about by the breath of rumor, to
make of them a constant theme of discussion. Is
not this what happens every day? I do undoubtedly
desire that a woman should be able to talk well of
dress, flowers, fruit, and of everything relating to the
management of her house; I should also wish her

[1] De la Ville, ch. vi. p. 289.

not to be ignorant of local affairs, and that she should possess at least an elementary knowledge of science to save her from the shoals of inexperience. But while I readily make all rational allowance for what is required by your position and the obligations of society, I still ask you would it not be possible, would it not be better, to elevate the tone of your conversations, and infuse into them more dignity and gravity of thought? Can Christian women find no interesting and lofty topics, attractive through their nobleness and simplicity, on which to converse? It seems to me, that with your quick and penetrating intellect it ought not to be difficult to change your present style of chattering into animated yet serious conversation, adorned with wisdom and geniality, thus causing life to flow between banks of flowers. "The words of the mouth of a wise man are grace." [1] If women rightly understood their social relations, they could create in every city centres of refined, enlightened, and agreeable society, where intellect would be cultivated, souls soothed, and the public mind find its best education. Men would then remain more contentedly in their homes, and be less tempted to leave them, because they would meet with something more than mere frivolity in their wives' conversation; they would insensibly become more polished and more refined by means of this constant intercourse, and this wholesome and reciprocal influence would be one of the great advantages of family and social life. Then what might be really called life would exist everywhere; an intellectual, thoughtful,

[1] Eccles. x. 12.

and Christian life, attractive in itself, and fruitful in good works, and with that life, an animated interest in everything; so that we should no longer be forced to concur in M. de Tocqueville's definition of worldly intercourse. He says — " The duties of society may be defined as an obligation existing in civilized society of mutually boring and inconveniencing each other. To whom has it not many times happened to find himself compelled to go and see a person who bored him, in order that he, in his turn, should come to his house and be equally bored."[1] This picture may be a little overdrawn; but has it not some foundation in truth? Of course many causes may be assigned for the *ennui* attached to those often artificial relations; but is not one of the chief this absence of everything serious and which possesses real interest? A hash of all the pettiness, vanity, and trifles of worldly life is daily served up in conversation; and is it possible that such food should not prove heavy and injurious to any rational being, whose understanding must be worn out and stifled under such a mass of confused and undefined nonentities?

III.

You must not imagine, when I thus strongly recommend gravity in conversation, that I desire to banish from it cheerfulness and innocent mirth. Nothing can be further from my intention, or from Christian teaching. St. Basil, when addressing his

[1] Corresp. vol. ii. p. 303.

monks, and laying down rules for their guidance during the hours of recreation, does not hesitate to say — "Let your conversation be full of grace and ease, . . . let it shed a pleasant perfume on the soul, and cheer it doubly, by the pleasure it gives and by the attraction of its wisdom."[1] "To practise virtue in conversation," wrote St. Francis of Sales to his nuns, "it is necessary to contribute your share of holy, equable cheerfulness, and of that pleasant, agreeable chat which may tend to the solace and recreation of your neighbor ; and never to cause them annoyance by frowning, melancholy countenances."[2] Do not forget that these counsels are written by Saints Basil and Francis of Sales for persons destined to the austere life of the cloister ; with how much greater reason, then, may I apply them to persons living in the world. St. Thomas gives the name of *eutrapélie* to the virtue of affability, that which promotes gayety and joyousness in our intercourse with our neighbors, and censures in rather severe terms those who refuse to contribute to the mirth of others by innocent pleasantry.[3] Why have the saints so often employed their pens in placing this advice before us ? Because the subject, from a religious point of view, is much more important than it appears to be at first sight. Nothing is so sure an indication of real virtue, nothing attracts others so much to the practice of virtue, as that cordial graciousness of manner which St. Anselm terms, "the perfume

---

[1] Constit. cap. xii. vol. ii. p. 798, edit. Gaume.
[2] 4 Entret. vol. i. p. 587.
[3] Vitiosi sunt et dicuntur duri et agrestes, 2a, 2æ, q. 168, art. 4.

of heavenly, undying happiness."[1] Cultivate a close union with hearts devoted to God, and whom He fills with His glory and His goodness; the mild, attractive virtue of such natures, imbued with the Divinity, their calmness and serenity will insensibly communicate themselves to you, and prepare your own hearts for the reception of heavenly light. And therefore, my children, far from desiring that you should become austere and melancholy in your social relations, I wish to see you, on the contrary, always manifesting a holy cheerfulness, and giving cordial vent to that natural, pleasant mirth, which is like the outpouring of a fresh, abundant spring. A celebrated commentator of the Bible says that "conversation should be agreeable, flowing, courteous, cheerful, and seasoned with Attic salt and hilarity."[2] St. Francis of Sales wished to see his penitents take their place among the best dressed women in society, and I should wish to see them also amongst the most joyous; and, in so speaking, I am only annotating the spirit of all the writings of the holy Bishop of Geneva. Let us suppose that in a city there are several, nay, many pious women, who never present "that sour and melancholy look" of which St. Francis speaks, but who, on the contrary, have joy sparkling on their lips, and the happiness virtue confers manifesting itself in the sweet and smiling expression of their countenances, for, like the Divine Wisdom, "they show themselves cheerfully in the way."[3]

---

[1] Quoted by Cornelius à Lapide, in Epist. ad Col. iv. 8.
[2] Quoted by Cornelius à Lapide, in Prov. xvi. 21, p. 433.
[3] Wisdom vi. 17.

And such holy women will often effect more good with their gracious cordiality and kindliness of manner than all the preachers in the world. Virtue, in all her splendor, seems to have borrowed their physiognomies in order to make herself visible to men; and the sight of genuine, sincere piety, thus adorned with heavenly graces, is the most powerful magnet for attracting souls to God. The Holy Scriptures somewhere say — "He shall kiss the lips who answereth right words." [1] Yes, kind, gentle, charitable words have all the tenderness of a mother's caress; they purify and ennoble the heart, pointing out to it the road to Heaven. May you, my children, have often on your lips those words which possess this double power of purifying and attracting souls, charming them and adorning them with angelic wings. May virtue daily draw to itself whatever gifts nature has endowed you with, in order to ennoble them, to shield them from the dangers of the world, and convert them into an element of happiness and perfection for others!

I will conclude with charity. Charity is the most necessary, yet perhaps the rarest, virtue in conversation. Charity in speech, in looks, even in silence — for there is a silence full of gall, which can scatter itself abroad without speaking a word; charity in insinuations, judgments, appreciation of others, hints, and reticence. It is of course often allowable, and even sometimes necessary, to speak of your neighbor's faults, in certain circumstances which prudence will point out; but then it must be always done with

---

[1] Prov. xxiv. 26.

moderation and right feeling, avoiding bitterness and every sentiment bordering on hate. But, as a general rule, we should respect the absent, treating others as we would wish them to treat us, for this is an eminently wise and Christian maxim. For if it happens that you hear you have been ill-spoken of in your absence, what annoyance does it not cause you? You feel as though you were suffering martyrdom and being burned alive. You tremble with indignation, and the blood boils in your veins.[1] Why have you, then, two different weights and measures? Why that readiness to wound others, and, on the other hand, why that suppressed irritation or violent outbreak when some one has merely scratched you? Let us respect the absent. I do not now mean to forbid those innocent jokes and that merry satire which often causes laughter at others' expense. They are the salt of conversation, and cross-grained minds only could take offence at them. I merely advise a certain degree of caution in such matters, for the descent is easy from innocent raillery to ill-natured remarks, and you may quickly glide down it, leaving all kindly feelings behind. "Injurious words," says one of the ancients, "are more terrible than a sword; for a sword can only wound the body, whereas words transfix the soul."[2] How many Christians are there, and often pious ones, who deceive themselves grossly on this head. They truly swallow iniquity like water, and perhaps one day, in place of the glorious

---

[1] "The most wicked people are precisely those who resent censure most." — Seneca, on Anger, bk. iii. ch. xxxvii.

[2] Pythagoras, Frag. Philos. Græ. vol. i. p. 496, edit. Didot.

crown they dreamed of, they will undergo a severe condemnation for their want of charity.

Should you have to listen to any such conversations, so grievously contrary to the first of Christian virtues, but which are so frequent in this world, follow the Wise Man's maxim : let them die within you, stifle all remembrance of them in your heart, that they may not take root therein, working disturbance in your soul. "Hast thou heard a word against thy neighbor? Let it die within thee, trusting that it will not burst thee." [1] There is a way of stifling all evil speaking : taking it as the offspring of the serpent, and crushing it instantly under the heel of an unswerving conscience, for then the soul is free and continues its route.

Observe towards all persons with whom you converse those two rules of courtesy and kindness. Make use of all those delicate attentions which give pleasure; seek to bring into relief your neighbor's good qualities, and avoid wounding his self-love. Know how to be silent in your turn and listen to others, especially when you are conversing with persons whose flow of speech is not easily stopped, but pours itself forth like the overflowing waters of a well. A little deference towards even a palpable weakness is often a proof of tact and goodness. Then will those beautiful words of Holy Writ be applied to you — "Before a storm goeth lightning, and before shamefacedness goeth favor, and for thy reverence good grace shall come to thee." [2]

Charity will also induce you to avoid discussion

[1] Ecclus. xix. 10. [2] Ecclus. xxxii. 14.

with those obstinate,[1] argumentative minds whose
opinions are all fixedly determined on beforehand,
and habitually present themselves to your notice with
the sharpest points and angles. Argument with
such characters is utterly useless for the purpose of
influencing them, and is also very hurtful, since it
can only degenerate into angry disputes. La Bruyere says of them that "they butt on every side like
rams. Can you expect to find rams without horns?
. . . The best thing to be done when you see them
in the distance is to fly from them with all speed, and
never look behind you. There are some people of
such a peculiar character and disposition, that it is
safest never to commit one's self with them, and to
complain as little as possible of what they do, for
they will never allow that you can be in the right."[2]
To butt against these rams is to expose one's self to
evident collisions, for such minds listen to nothing,
because they cannot see nor understand anything
but their own ideas. They are like cannon-balls,
always rushing onwards in a straight line; the best
thing to be done is to slip aside, or if that cannot
easily be accomplished, to oppose to them the inertia
of patience and the calm wisdom of charity.

Two words more, two pieces of advice, which may
be looked on as the perfume of this discourse. If
you can do so simply, without sermonizing, say some-

[1] "Nevertheless, a gentle contradiction sometimes lends animation
to discourse. The reparteee of one of the ancients to his ever constant, monotonous applauder is well known: 'Contradict me, pray,
that we may differ about something.' " — Seneca, on Anger, bk. iii. ch.
viii.

[2] De la Société, ch. v. p. 271.

thing for the glory of God, speak some little pious word, and rest assured that nothing will suffer by doing so,—neither your wit, nor your reputation, nor the charm of your conversation. There must be nothing affected, nothing stilted, no preparation, no studied effects; but when a really religious mind speaks freely, something divine is sure to drop from the lips, and the holy thought finds its way into the listener's heart, all the more surely and efficaciously that it is a seed which has almost unconsciously fallen from the tree which bore it. A single word uttered thus at hazard may lead to the conversion of a soul, and guide it gently back into the paths of virtue and holiness. Have you not remarked how often you have come back from worldly conversations with your mind fatigued, soul empty, heart dissatisfied, and tone of character deteriorated? When you return home withdraw immediately into the sanctuary of your own heart; there pray in secret, hold converse with yourself, but still more with God. Delicious and satisfying communion! You will there revive both body and soul in that spiritual bath taken after the heat of the day. It was the counsel of the Wise Man; I leave it you as the conclusion of this discourse — "When I go into my house, I shall repose myself with her, for her conversation hath no bitterness, nor her company any tediousness, but joy and gladness." [1]

---

[1] Wisdom viii. 16.

SIXTH DISCOURSE.

ENVY AND JEALOUSY.

"For we ourselves were also some time living in malice and envy, hateful, hating one another." — TITUS iii. 3.

THERE is a vice which in Holy Scripture is always classed with hatred, dissension, deceit, and all great crimes; it is that of envy and jealousy. "From whence are wars and contentions among you?" says St. James. "Are they not hence, from your concupiscences, which war in your members? You covet, and have not; you kill, and envy, and cannot obtain. You contend and war, and you have not, because you ask not."[1] The Apostle St. Peter holds the same language — "Wherefore, my brethren, laying away all malice, and all guile, and dissimulations, and envies, and all detractions."[2] "By the envy of the devil," says the Wise Man, "death came into the world; and they follow him that are of his side."[3] "It was this vice," St. Augustine writes, "which drove Adam out of Paradise, killed Abel, kindled the hatred of his brethren against Joseph, and cast Daniel into the lion's den. . . . My brethren, preach it aloud every-

[1] St. James iv. 1, 2.　　[2] 1 St. Peter ii. 1.　　[3] Wisdom ii. 24, 25.

where, even on the house-tops, that envy is a wild beast which destroys all trust, ruins concord, frustrates justice, and engenders every species of evil."[1]

I have formed the design of giving you some instructions respecting envy and jealousy; as I think there is no more practical subject to be found, nor one richer in details. These passions play an immense and a daily part in man's life, continually modifying his thoughts and desires, and influencing his feelings, projects, and conduct, while they are also one of the chief sources of all our agitations and anxieties.[2] And might it not, too, be said that it is they who raise the principal storms in women's lives — in the inner life of their hearts and minds, in that of their thoughts and actions? I shall devote three of our meetings to this subject, and shall take the definition, description, and frequency of this vice as the matter of my first discourse.

I.

I shall commence with the definition. To define, means to mark out the limits of an idea, to circumscribe it within its true bounds, and take from it everything not belonging to it. A clear definition of a question is sometimes all that is required to resolve it, or, at all events, to prepare the materials for an easy solution.

---

[1] St. Augustine, quoted by Cornelius à Lapide, in Epist. 1 St. Peter ii. p. 630.

[2] St. Gregory Thaumaturgus, in Ecclus. iv. p. 998, edit. Migné.

Let us first determine the meaning of those three words — envy, jealousy, and emulation. Envy and jealousy are two terms often mistaken for each other, two passions proceeding from the same root, and often intertwined one with the other, like the branches of those crooked trees in the environs of Rheims, called "the beeches of Verzy,"[1] where you see the branches starting from different points of the same trunk, then turning towards each other, till they meet and become confounded in one, when they again separate, to meet again further on. And so of envy and jealousy; they are two branches springing from the same root of pride and cupidity. When you seek to define them, they are evidently very different, but if you follow them through the windings of the heart, and the daily habits of life, you will often find them confounded together; one is mistaken for the other, and they are called by one name or the other indifferently. And the reason of it is, because their points of contact so easily unite, and because in their motions they alternate so quickly with every impulse of the heart. For this reason, it will often happen in the course of these instructions that one of these passions will take the place of the other, and be called by the general name of envy or jealousy. La Bruyere has already remarked this, for he says — "Jealousy is never exempt from some tinge of envy, and these two passions are even often mistaken for each other."[2]

Yet there is in our minds a very distinct and

---

[1] Beeches with distorted branches twisted one over the other.
[2] De l'Homme, ch. xi. p. 325.

marked shade of difference between envy and jealousy. You feel jealous of your own possessions, envious of those of others. "Jealousy," says La Rochefoucauld, "wishes to retain something belonging to ourselves, or which we think ought to belong to us; while envy is a sort of madness which cannot endure to witness the prosperity of others."[1] There is some one who is richer and more considered in society than yourself, and you are troubled at it; you feel humiliated and pained by the sense of your own inferiority, and you would willingly strip such a person of the esteem and good fortune he enjoys in order to enrich yourself with his spoils. That is a sin of envy. Again, such a one is wittier, and above all she is a greater beauty, — yes, even a greater beauty than yourself. Oh the wretches that dare give utterance to such an impertinence! Do they not know they are putting you on the rack, showing you no pity, and exciting a storm of envy in your heart! You possess some authority, and others repose a certain amount of confidence in you; but you cannot be satisfied unless all this devolves wholly and entirely on yourself, and cannot bear that others should share it with you, even though they may be legitimately entitled to do so. In this case you may be said to be jealous of authority and the esteem of others. You are so exclusive in your affections that you carry a feeling of jealousy into all your relations with others, and thus embitter them for yourself and others. When the feeling of jealousy is properly directed and restrained within due limits, it may be sometimes

[1] Maxims, xxviii. p. 153, edit. Didot.

lawful. Thus we may, and, speaking in the truest
sense, we ought to feel jealous of our rights and
authority, provided that we are not exclusive in the
matter, and do not step beyond the bounds of our
real rights; for if we do, we shall simply fall into the
very fault with which we reproach others; for where
the line of our authority ends, that of our neighbor
begins. Therefore, when I speak of jealousy in these
discourses, I always mean that which is unreasonable,
excessive, and ill-regulated.

Along with envy and jealousy we find another
feeling, good, laudable, useful, and even necessary, —
that of emulation. Emulation is a great and generous
impulse of mind and heart, inspired by the sight of
what is admirable and praiseworthy in our neighbor,
and which incites us to acquire that good in which
we ourselves are deficient, but without any wish to
deprive others of what they possess. Emulation is
a source of life and fruitfulness; it is man's free will
exerting itself to obtain perfection in the sphere of
good. Emulation is the general law of all beings;
even horses, when harnessed together, mutually
excite each other to speed, or spurred to the race,
seem to devour space in their eagerness to keep the
foremost rank. "Emulation," writes St. Thomas,
"marches forward to the conquest of good, but envy
mourns because it cannot take possession of the
treasures of others."[1] And the holy Doctor, as well

---

[1] Aristotle's words have not been quite literally rendered. Aristotle, Rhetor. bk. ii. ch. xi. p. 362, edit. Didot: Ad invidere improbum
est, et hominum improborum — "But it is a wicked thing to envy, and
it is the part of wicked men."

as the philosopher, defines emulation as a quality
appertaining to the virtuous man, and envy as the
strife of the wicked. St. Jerome, speaking to a
Roman lady about her daughter's education, said,
"She should have companions towards whom she can
feel emulation, that the praises bestowed on them
may excite her own efforts." [1]

When I find fault with envy and jealousy, my censures are never meant to be directed against that
noble emulation in doing good, of which St. Paul
writes, "Be zealous for the better gifts." [2] And
again, "Be zealous for that which is good in a good
thing always.[3]

II.

St. Gregory the Great and St. Basil have left us
description of envy and jealousy, which perhaps
would not be always applicable to the people of these
countries as far as exterior marks go, for our northern
races are colder and less expressive in their gestures ;
but their interior feelings lose nothing· in intensity,
as the volcano burns all the fiercer beneath its covering of snow.[4] I will let these holy Doctors speak;
the description and oratorical analysis which has
been traced by their learned pens will complete the
definition I have given you. "When the heart,"

---

[1] Quoted by St. Thomas, De Malo, q. 10, art. i. vol. xv. pp. 182–
184.

[2] 1 Cor. xii. 31.   [3] Gal. iv. 18.

[4] "Man," writes Hesiod, "has for his constant companion Envy,
with her malevolent tongue, repulsive countenance, and joy in evil
only." — Trav. et Jours. ch. v. pp. 195, 196, edit. Didot.

says St. Gregory, "is attacked by this malady, the external symptoms soon attest its gravity. A pallid hue spreads itself over the countenance, the eyes are cast down, the mind is troubled, and the agitation often communicates itself to every member of the body. Such persons can enjoy nothing, because they are eating away their own hearts, and every success gained by their neighbor is a source of suffering to them."[1] "The envious and the jealous are easily recognized by their physiognomy," writes St. Basil. "Their eyes are dull and heavy, their jaws drooping, their brows contracted, their mind agitated and wanting judgment in their appreciation of others. They can see no good in acts of virtue, nor in eloquent words, nor in anything which the world admires. Vultures leave sweet-smelling meadows for the attraction of putrid carrion, and flies throng round festering wounds. In like manner the envious man does not stop and dwell on the beauty and greatness of good deeds, but turns to their defective aspect; and as imperfection is to be met with in everything, he delights in divulging it, and seeks to make this imperfection the characteristic mark of his neighbor. . . . Besides this, envious men are very skilful in giving a bad appearance to what is good in itself, and in calumniating virtue by speaking of it as bordering on vice. They call a determined man audacious and rash, and a temperate one cold-blooded; with them justice is cruelty; prudence, cunning; liberality, prodigality; and a wise administration, parsimony."[2]

[1] Moral, bk. v. ch. xlvi. p. 728, vol. i.
[2] De Invid. n. 5, vol. iii. p. 382.

III.

Envy and jealousy are vices which unfortunately are everywhere to be met with. Cicero complained of them in his time — "The greater number of men are envious, for there is no more common nor universal vice."[1] Christianity, the religion of charity and humility, ought, one would say, to have notably lessened this vice, if it did not altogether do away with it. Has that been its effect? Listen to the reply of St. Chrysostom, and if you deem it unsatisfactory, recollect that the fault does not lie with the teaching of Christianity, but with those persons who call themselves Christians — "I would truly wish to be silent, . . . but the facts themselves cry out too loudly for me, and there will be some advantage gained by denouncing this vice. This evil has insinuated itself into the Church, and thrown everything into disorder. . . . We are always waging war against each other, and it is envy that places the weapons in our hands. These have for results a general depravity, . . . and if every one labors to destroy the edifice, what is to be the end of it?"[2] Behold the truth, my children, as these great masters of the faith knew how to tell it. Their earnest, ardent words found their way everywhere into church and sanctuary, in order to scourge those vices which often sought to hide behind the pillars of the temple, or beneath the shadow of the altar. Yes; envy and jealousy are almost universal plague-spots, disfiguring humanity,

[1] De Orat. bk. ii. ch. lii. p. 259, vol. i.
[2] In Epist. 2 ad Cor. hom. xxvii. vol. x. p. 749.

and too often even that portion of it which has been regenerated by Christ. They are counted amongst the capital sins, according to the teaching of the great Doctors of the Church, and yet they creep in everywhere, and contrive to form a union with all that is most sacred, — with frequent communion and austere practices of piety. They are found in every confraternity, and often in the post of honor at religious meetings, for how could the meeting be held in the absence of such a saint? Alas! my children, these comedies are not as rare as they ought to be; no wonder they are a source of amusement to infidels and men of the world, who smile and shrug their shoulders, and not without reason, when they witness all those petty intrigues at the side-scenes. Where they err is in making religion responsible for all the littleness and miseries of humanity.

"There are more disinterested than unenvious people in the world,"[1] says La Rochefoucald. And yet, my children, the number of disinterested people in this world is very small. Self-interest, and immoderate attachment to the goods of this life, are epidemics which have always more or less prevailed here below. This is a fact, and yet the moralist is not wrong in asserting that the unenvious are still rarer. Talent, wealth, beauty, position in society, the esteem enjoyed by others, the place they hold, either in public opinion or in their relations to others, — all these serve as food for envy and jealousy. And for this cause, people find it much easier to obtain pardon for their faults than for their virtues; for any

---

[1] Maxims, cccclxxxvi. p. 178.

good quality, like a ray of light, reveals the inferiority of others; and, in the eyes of some people, this is an unpardonable crime. Your virtue is an indirect reproach to them. Your failings, on the contrary, throw into relief whatever they deem worthy of admiration in their own character; so, the more you possess, the more gracious they are. But you must never venture to claim that particular good quality or virtue, which apparently tends to diminish what they consider their own special perfection. That would be a crime in their eyes, implying, according to them, a censure on their inferiority. " He is become a censurer of our thoughts." [1]

There are some proud, egotistical, envious natures in this world, with whom it seems a necessity to decry others, to implant a sting, and leave the mark of their teeth in everything good. Speak to them of the beauty of Rheims Cathedral, and they will remark how unfortunate it is that the statue over the portal should have its nose mutilated. Tell them that such a one is good, upright, and charitable, and they will instantly come out with some unfounded piece of gossip they have accidentally picked up somewhere or other, in order to diminish at least your good opinion of him. A German philosopher spoke in the following terms, of a lady of his acquaintance — " I have now twice met Madame de la Roche, and find her just the same person she was at twenty, — just as prone to decry others, always exalting the commonplace, and vilifying everything great and eminent; dressing up all topics with a sauce of her own making, and

---

[1] Wisdom ii. 14.

inviting you to regale yourself with it." [1] How faithful and exact a description ? How many such sneering characters do we not meet in this world, and how
many mediocre and evilly-disposed persons, who seek,
with the force of their own wickedness, to hammer
down to the level of their own inferiority all that is
superior to them. They exalt the commonplace; and
when doing so, it is themselves whom they are secretly seeking to enhance, for all that is commonplace
is their proper element. They vilify goodness and
greatness, for, whatever is eminent seems a reproach
to them, and a reflection on their mediocrity and
folly. And what is most deplorable is, that these
sowers of discord can always find ears sufficiently
credulous or malicious to give credit to their tales.
"Thus," says St. Chrysostom, "is the Church of
Christ continually agitated and disturbed."

Ah ! if the minds of Christians were filled with
great and noble ideas; if their intellects were enlightened with the light of faith, their hearts inflamed
with the ardors of charity, the bias of their characters formed on the model of the great saints of the
primitive Church, would they have time to trouble
themselves about these petty things, or leisure to
occupy themselves with all these miserable trifles ?
Piety is, unfortunately, too often made an affair of
outward forms and observances, and religion is cut
down to suit the ideas of narrow-minded, petty souls;
while behind this screen of exterior forms and practices we find all the trivialities and the formidable
passions of suspicious, jealous, spiteful, and vindictive

[1] Goethe, Corresp. avec Schiller, vol. ii. p. 114.

minds, who tear their neighbor's character to shreds
with the hypocritical smoothness of a plausible
tongue. Such people permit themselves to do many
things which revolt the consciences of all good and
liberal-minded men, and thus alienate true hearts and
do much harm to religion. The Scripture says that
envy is the vice of little minds: "Envy slayeth the
little one." Ah! if Christians had ideas worthy of
their holy calling, their hearts would be filled only
with a noble emulation for good.

Speaking of the frequency of jealousy, I must
make some special observations to you, which you
will permit me to do with the frankness inspired by
my paternal affection for you.

We find beside each of our good qualities, innate
tendencies, and lawful aspirations, — a corresponding
defect. Woman has her special qualities, virtues,
and mission in this world. She is the beauteous
flower of her family and of society, formed to please.
Like the verdant ivy, she attaches herself to some
support, in order to mount upwards, so that the essential point for her welfare and happiness is to make
a good choice in that support to which she clings.
Woman, then, is chiefly influenced through the heart,
which is one reason why she is more prone to jealousy than man. Yes, my children, all moralists declare that women are, from their nature, more easily
rendered jealous; and even in default of this testimony from moralists, must you not yourselves bear
witness that the assertion is true? A woman is
naturally jealous; sometimes jealous of every one —
of her husband, her children, married and unmarried,

and of her friends. Jealous of all who have more wit or beauty, or who enjoy more consideration. Her fickle heart and lively imagination do, or may, create for her under this head a whole crowd of chimeras which have no more reality than the fevered dreams of an invalid. I have known women a prey to a slow, consuming, constant fever, which was secretly undermining both soul and body, transfixing them to a bed of suffering, and feeding them with imaginary grievances. The name of this fever was jealousy. Fatal disease, everywhere met with, and for which the physician's aid is so seldom sought!

May God preserve you, my children, from it! Love Him with all your hearts; take your stand on the mountains of truth, and sustain your souls with the mild and radiant light of faith. Let the great revelations of Christianity be the horizon of your minds, and make not the narrow valleys of this world your resting-place. Let not your piety resemble the servant who refuses the public entrance into a garden, in order that the proprietor may reserve to himself alone the power of watching over its precincts, and cultivating therein, under the guise of celestial plants, the seeds of many earthly passions. Cultivate instead noble and generous sentiments, nourish both mind and heart with holy thoughts, worthy of your dignity as children of God; then you will not easily stoop to the meanness of jealousy, for that is a specialty of petty minds and narrow hearts — "Envy slayeth the little one." [1]

[1] Job v. 2.

SEVENTH DISCOURSE.

ENVY AND JEALOUSY.

CONTINUED.

"From whence are wars and contentions among you? . . . you kill, and envy, and cannot obtain." — ST. JAMES iv. 1, 2.

I HAVE undertaken to treat a very delicate, and especially practical subject in the lives of women — envy and jealousy. Prone as this passion is to take a hundred different forms, how shall I best describe it? How shall I seize on the ever-varying lights and shades of the picture, so as to bring it perfectly before you? This question reminds me of the story of Proteus. Here it is, as Virgil relates it: "When you have caught him, says Cyrene to the shepherd Aristæus, he will seek to elude your grasp by taking a hundred various shapes and figures of wild beasts. You may see him suddenly turn into a grisly bear, an enraged tiger, a scaly dragon, and a lioness with tawny mane; or perchance he will escape your bonds in the form of a sparkling, crackling flame; or again, as a stream of running water, he will flow from between your hands. But the greater the number of figures he assumes, the more closely you must bind your chains, . . . and then he will be glad to answer your questions."[1] I do not know if I shall be as fortunate as the shepherd Aristæus in binding this Proteus of human passions which we call envy and jealousy. But I shall at least try to do so, and, indeed, I have already tried in my last discourse. After having defined these two vices, and drawn a distinction between them and another feeling, which is both a noble and a generous one, that of emulation, I translated for you some sentences from the Fathers of the Church, where the portraits of envy and jealousy are presented to us in strong relief, and with the liveliest colors. I also proved to you how common those vices are, how almost universally spread throughout the world,[2] even the religious world; and how they demand special mention when speaking of the lives of women.

I will devote to-day to examining into these two points — the causes and effects of envy and jealousy.

I.

The sources of envy and jealousy must always be bad. I am not now alluding to that pardonable jealousy of our lawful rights and privileges; I am speaking only of the evil and ill-regulated phases of the passion.

Our Creator, and still more our Redeemer, have liberally placed at our disposal all the really desirable

---

[1] Georg. iv. 405, 408.
[2] "Invidis referta sunt omnia." — Cicero, Orat. cap. xli.

goods of this world. If virtue, industry, and order rule a family, the necessaries of life are rarely wanting; and even if they should fail in some exceptional cases, Providence comes to the relief. It would be easy for me to prove that, according to the ordinary laws of nature, virtue here below will always find not only enough, but even a superabundance, of all the temporal goods necessary for our pilgrimage and for the dignity suitable to our position in life. "Seek ye first the Kingdom of God, and His justice, and all things else shall be added unto you."[1] True good, according to the moral law, consists in moderating your desires, in the practice of virtue, in love of God, and in all those treasures of heart and intellect which Christianity places at your disposal. But all these riches may be yours, if you wish it; the only limit being your own good-will, aided by the grace of God. If your hearts are filled with love of God; if your souls are at peace; if your desires are restrained within due bounds; if you are contented with your lot, you will never be exposed to the temptation of envy; or should you ever be, you will be able to overcome it very easily.[2] Spiritual goods may be indefinitely distributed, without suffering any diminution; therefore the accumulated treasures of our neighbor do not hinder us from enriching ourselves.

Whence, then, comes envy? From Pride, which loves to rule over all, and bring every one to her feet;

---

[1] St. Matt. vi. 32.

[2] "Man would never be envious, were his desires moderate, and in keeping with his character." — Alibert, Physiolog. des Passions, vol. i. p. 339.

and from Vanity, which is pained at the idea of not occupying the place to which, according to herself, she is entitled. It has its source in the unbridled desires of a soul which is never satisfied with its own lot, but is always seeking for more, and ambitioning what it does not possess, and what it probably is the intention of Providence it shall never possess. "Whence are wars and contentions among you? you kill, and envy, and cannot obtain."[1] Ah, my children, if the true causes of the envy that some people manifest were published, they would be covered with confusion. Some one said to me one day — "Why does such a one dislike that person so much? She never misses an opportunity of slandering, or, at all events, of sneering at her." "You wish to know the reason," I said; "well, then, here it is: I will tell it you." And I unfolded to her a long story of hidden ambition, disappointed vanity, and absurd pretension on one side; and on the other, the honest simplicity of an upright mind, which, compelled by circumstances, and the sincerity of a real friendship, had been forced to set itself against wishes which could never be realized. When I had finished my story my questioner looked utterly petrified, and then exclaimed — "It is really enough to make one blush for human nature!" What a number of similar stories would come to light if we knew all; if we could raise that heavy curtain which conceals the true, but hidden, face of men and things! Generally speaking, when you see any one belonging to that company of sharp-shooters who are always

---

[1] St. James iv. 1, 2.

ready to let fly darts and arrows against their neighbors, and more especially against some one particular
person, say to yourself, May there not be, behind all
this, some story of wounded pride, secret jealousy,
or embittered self-love? You may answer, Yes, beforehand, and you will rarely find yourself wrong.
" They that held darts provoked him, and quarrelled
with him, and envied him." [1] Or you may also say,
there is some secret history here, like that of Joseph
sold by his brethren, and the recital of it cannot be
very edifying to hear. " His brethren, therefore, envied him." [2]

There remains a very delicate question to be
treated of, where it is not easy to follow out the
shades of thought through all their different colors.
Does jealousy, even that jealousy which is lawful,
always proceed from love? Here are the answers of
certain moralists, which I will give you word for
word. " There is more self-love than real love in
jealousy." [3] And another writes — " Jealousy is only
a proof of little love, foolish pride, and enforced ac-
knowledgment of one's own want of merit, and even,
sometimes, of a bad heart." [4] Please to reflect on
what you know of the secret stories of women's
hearts, and perhaps you will allow that there is some
truth in the words of these moralists. The words
heart, feelings, and affections, play a great part in
the programme of life, but their actual existence is
rare enough. The vanity of such a one has been
hurt, but she does not like it, and so she says her

---

[1] Gen. xlix. 23.   [2] Gen. xxxvi. 11.
[3] La Rochefoucauld, Maxims, cccxxiv. p. 171.   [4] Duclos.

heart has been wounded. It sounds better, more touching, and so this false coin is often presented to the public; but, to do them justice, though politely accepted, it is rarely believed in. Such another is of a jealous disposition, which often happens without feeling affection for others; but she likes to possess their confidence — at least, to appear to do so; she looks on that as men do on a decoration for merit, and now some unforeseen accident has deprived her of the distinction. With hand on her heart, she moans, and pretends that it is cruelly wounded. Ah, no! her heart has never been touched; it is only her vanity, which suffers from the destruction of her plans for the future. What can I say more? You wish for nothing more — the heart alone. Ah, my children, the heart, really the heart, that is, faithful and disinterested affection, becomes known in certain trying circumstances, which are the touchstone of real, sincere attachments. It is then we discover that pure and sterling metal which we call the heart. It sends forth flashes of bright, fiery electricity, free from all dross of worldly interests. We recognize the diamond by the manner in which it reflects the rays of light! But in the majority of cases the heart is a word too often profaned, and made to serve as a cloak for self-interest, pride, vanity, and ambition. I knew a mother who would have preferred seeing her daughter unhappy in one position than happy in another, merely because that was less flattering to her maternal vanity. And that mother professed to be devoted to her daughter! It is a mere jugglery of words to try and make the most thorough and the blindest selfishness pass for disinterested attachment!

Let us now consider the effects of this deplorable passion.

II.

Envy and jealousy are the most terrible and the most violent of human passions. They poison individual lives, bring discord into families, and have more than once wrought disturbances in empires. I may assert, without fear of being contradicted by experience, that many individual and social misfortunes, and a very large number of crimes, are due to these two fatal passions.

It is a gnawing worm which dwells in the viewless regions of the soul and devours its own substance, causing acute pain all the while. The greater number of passions allow us some little repose, — once satisfied they grow calm, at least for a little while; but envy and jealousy consume the heart unceasingly, and become more energetic the more they are indulged. Look at that woman, to whose happiness nothing seems wanting: an honored position, suitable fortune, sincere affection, — all these does she possess. Only one thing is wanting to her, and that is to compare her lot with that of others, and enjoy with gratitude the blessings which God has given her. But she does not; her heart is consumed by the slow, gnawing fever of envy, and her veins are filled with liquid fire. The sight of a happiness which seems greater than her own; of a position which commands more respect; the idea of being inferior to any one else in the advantages of mind and body, — all these are so many spectres to mar her enjoyment, and embitter all the goods which fortune has provided for her. For this cause, when the Fathers of the Church speak of this vice, they scarcely know what comparisons to use that shall be strong enough to express their idea, and they consequently heap them on each other in rich luxuriance, in order to explain their meaning. St. Chrysostom says, "Moths and worms do not eat into wool and wood with so much persistency as envy gnaws the entrails of those who suffer from the attacks of that passion."[1]   "A serpent within a human body will not prey on that body if it is given other and sufficient nourishment, but everything is good for envy,; it gnaws, it bites, it devours, and tears the soul to pieces, and there is no power of calming its fury."[2]   St. Basil says, "Envy is the most dangerous of our passions and the worst of evils; and the fact of its being a domestic evil only adds weight to its gravity. Rust consumes iron, and envy consumes the heart. The viper when born rends the entrails of its mother, and envy in like manner destroys the soul that gives it birth."[3]

When a soul falls under her melancholy influence, it sees everything through the medium of this passion. It invents a hundred chimeras, and lives in a waking dream; it takes the veriest trifles as certain

[1] Eclog. de Invidia, vol. xii. p. 727.
[2] Chrysostom, in Epist. ii. ad Cor. Hom. xxvii. vol. x. p. 745.
[3] De Invidia, vol. iii. pp. 371–374.

proofs, and looks on the most innocent occurrences as indisputable proofs. A grain of sand is a mountain in the eyes of envy; a leaf falling in the forest a witness not to be doubted. There is no passion which renders people so distrustful, susceptible, unjust, and suspicious as envy and jealousy. Consequently, as so many events in this world must remain in partial obscurity, if not in darkness, because some mystery must accompany a multitude of our actions, and as everything around us is full of hidden meanings, it follows that, if persons wish to torment themselves, they have plenty of opportunities for so doing. They can make a storm out of every cloud, and raise at will a tempest in their own souls.

This passion is so awful in its effects that it sometimes reacts violently, even on the body. The countenance grows pale, livid, and visibly thinner, while sadness perpetually clouds the expression, the looks, and the lips, because, like the waters of some bitter spring, it is constantly welling up from the depths of the heart. The happiness of others excites it, and seems to shrivel up the entire physical organization. "Paleness sits upon the brow,"[1] as the poet says. Books on medicine contain numerous and fearful revelations about the unhappy victims of this internal cancer. You have seen, and may see any day, persons slowly wasting away under the influence of this passion, until they die of consumption; for any fierce passion will wear out the body as certainly as an actual poison. "Envy and anger," says the Holy Ghost, "shorten a man's days. . . . But a cheerful

1 "Pallor in ore sedet. . . . intabescitque videndo."—Ovid.
10*

and good heart is always feasting, for his banquets are prepared with diligence."[1]

Holy Writ perfectly describes, in another place, the physical and moral results of this passion. "Wrath, envy, trouble, unquietness, and the fear of death, continual anger, and strife, and in the time of rest upon his bed, the sleep of the night changeth his knowledge. A little and as nothing is his rest, and afterwards in sleep, as in the day of keeping watch. He is troubled in the vision of his heart, as if he had escaped in the day of battle. In the time of his safety he rises up, and wondereth that there is no fear."[2] Think over the secret story of your own lives, my children — those histories into which romance always enters more or less — call up again your recollections, and say do you not recognize yourselves, at least in part, in this living animated sketch of the disquietudes, dreams, and phantoms, which harass and trouble human life, and whose chief source is jealousy.

This passion, also, completely alters the character and sours the mind, making you ill tempered and impossible to please. I have even seen some good and gentle dispositions quite metamorphosed by it, and becoming gloomy, sad, fretful, and unapproachable. Woman, in particular, loses her gentleness of character, graciousness of manner, and kindliness of disposition. She has no longer that tender, cloudless heart, nourished by goodness and affection, and revelling in a perpetual feast; but becomes a being apart, a strange mixture of liquid bitterness and

[1] Ecclus. xxx. 26, 27.   [2] Ecclus. xl. 4–7.

sugary sweetness turning sour. It is what the Scripture forcibly describes in the words — "Envy is the rottenness of the bones."[1] There is some sort of moral and physical decomposition in all this.

But this vice does not exercise its ravages only in men's minds; it is everywhere, and always found to be hard and pitiless as hell. Why is that family disunited? Why do hate and discord reign at that domestic hearth? If you could trace them back to their first source, you would find there almost to a certainty the gnawing worm of hate and jealousy. It was the canker which penetrated the root, gained entrance into the trunk, and ascended even to the branches of the tree. Whence came the death of Abel? From the envy which corroded his brother's heart, until that unhappy man could no longer bear to see him more esteemed than himself. Cain wanted to be wicked himself, and wished at the same time to prevent others from being good. This is the last stage, the very delirium, of the passion. Why was Joseph sold by his brethren? You know it was jealousy alone which dictated that bargain, and was the cause of that crime. And yet you, perhaps, are now indulging some secret hatred against another! Ah! let me implore of you not to seek for specious pretexts and plausible reasons. I know you are very ingenious at disguising your rancor under false colors, and finding out motives where none exist. You are like those courtiers, of whom St. Simon says that they endeavored to draw forth sighs from the very soles of their boots! You seek for accomplices

---

[1] Prov xiv. 30.

in your passion in the very people you take counsel with ; you have such a talent for gilding over your baseness, and giving it the very turn you wish ; you know how to manœuvre with such tact, that you necessarily get the very answer you desire.

All this proves the skill and cunning of this passion ; but in reality, here before God, answer truly — has not this person whom you are thus persecuting but one crime in your eyes, which crime may even be a virtue in the sight of God, but it gives umbrage to your jealousy ? That is the real reason ; all the rest are mere phantoms, which you may bring every one to believe in except your own conscience, which is aware of the truth, and God, to Whom all is known.

There is one species of jealousy which sometimes brings about the most deplorable results : that of a mother-in-law. A son or daughter is married ; if their mother be sensible, and a true Christian, she ought to understand that there exists a hierarchy of feeling and different spheres of affection, differing in their objects, but all capable of working together, and even of mutually aiding each other when combined. Thus a mother may perfectly well retain her share of her son or daughter's affection, while allowing the laws of the Creator to take their due course. Maternal love has its rights, but conjugal love has its also ; and it is written — "A man shall leave father and mother and cleave to his wife." When a mother bows to this law, and helps in carrying it out, she loses nothing, but may gain a great deal. Her children, seeing that their mother's love for them, far from making itself an obstacle, seeks to become an additional link in their mutual affection, will reflect back on her the genial warmth of their love, and the rights of filial piety will thus obtain a double portion, — that which is due to them in the natural order of things, and that which the gratitude of two happy hearts delights in pouring forth before them. With any one who has a right comprehension of these matters, the different degrees of affection, far from injuring, mutually uphold each other, like the stones in an arch. But some mothers cannot be got to understand this truth; their love is too exclusive and ill-regulated; it is a love which manifests itself only in unreasonable jealousy, thus often causing their own unhappiness and that of their children. I have known some who had nearly set young couples at variance for life, for while professing to love their children tenderly, they really loved themselves far more, almost exclusively; and it is one of the illusions of life, often wilfully indulged in, to persuade yourself, and to try to persuade others, that you love truly, while all the time this pretended affection is mere selfishness and jealousy. A true and sincere affection, like everything else in this world, is known by its acts, as the tree is known by its fruits.

Why, too, do we find, if we extend our horizon, empires disturbed, wars declared, and rivers of blood shed? Why do we see everywhere legacies of revenge and hatred handed down from people to people, and from generation to generation? The first sole cause has often been a jealous impulse; and, for all I know, perhaps only a woman's thirst for ven-

geance. I do not say that this wish for revenge was
the immediate cause of the deplorable results to
which I allude; but the tiny rivulet swelled by degrees
and widened, till it successively poisoned men's relations with others, gained more ground, became a
great flood, and overwhelmed with its inundations
the plains of humanity. Ah! I, too, must say, borrowing the idea of the Apostle — O thou little spark
of jealousy, what fierce and devastating fires thou
hast kindled in the course of ages. "Behold how
small a fire, what a great wood it kindleth!"[1]

In default of higher motives, the consideration of
the injury which this vice causes to yourselves, and
the ridicule which it draws down on you, ought to
effect its cure. Jealousy does most harm to the
jealous man himself.[2] He is its first and chief vic-
tim; his heart is gnawed by the vulture, like that of
Prometheus on the mountain. It is true he can cast
forth venom and poison those around him; but the
source of the poison is in his own heart, and puts
forth all its force first on himself. It also sometimes
happens that the person you wish to strike is one
whom circumstances or the strength of his own
character renders completely invulnerable to the
shafts of envy; and then, says St. Basil, "their darts
are like arrows shot from a powerful bow, which,
striking against a hard rock, recoil on the archer and
grievously wound him."[3]

---

[1] St. James iii. 5.

[2] "Malice drinks the greatest portion of its own venom." — Atta-
lus, quoted by Seneca, Epist. lxxxi.

[3] De Invidia, vol. iii. p. 579.

It is said that in France ridicule kills. I earnestly wish it could kill jealousy; and indeed it might well do so if jealous natures only knew how they are laughed at, how easily their supposed crafty schemes are seen through, and with what malicious enjoyment the discovery of the real reason of all their plots and mischief-making and slanders is hailed. Some one said once to Voltaire — "You are so intensely jealous that if it should ever enter your head to play at cooking, you would actually come to hate your own cook." [1] And you, too, are jealous — jealous to that extent that every one excites your distrust, every one becomes intolerable to you; so jealous that it is in vain you try to conceal it, and disguise this secret idol of your heart in the flowing draperies which you dignify with the name of rights and privileges. Rest assured no one is deceived. Each one whispers in his neighbor's ear the secret of the little comedy you are acting, for you have gone on the stage and are laughed at. That is all you have gained.

How much wiser it would be, my children, to cultivate a rational, Christian frame of mind! In that alone can we find peace of heart, — peace with God, peace with ourselves, and with men of good will.

[1] See Bescherelle, art. "Jealousy."

EIGHTH DISCOURSE.

ENVY AND JEALOUSY.

CONTINUED.

"But if you have bitter zeal, and there be contentions in your hearts, glory not, and be not liars against the truth. For this is not wisdom, descending from above, but earthly, sensual, devilish. For where envying and contention is, there is inconstancy and every evil work." — St. James iii. 14-16.

The cause of envy and jealousy is found in the root of all bad passions of the heart; it is there they have their starting-point, and there they develop themselves until they poison our lives, words, and actions. And what fearful ravages they occasion in individuals, in families, and in social life! The soul is devoured by an internal cancer, which causes acute suffering, and vitiates all the lawful enjoyment which the goods of nature and grace can bestow on it. It becomes suspicious, distrustful, and unjust; it sees evil in everything, until even the body also is attacked by the disease; the countenance grows pale and livid, and the whole constitution is often materially injured. The character changes, and the best dispositions grow melancholy, morose, and unapproachable. Domestic peace is disturbed, and affection, which ought to be the life of the heart and the greatest blessing that those who are united by the ties of blood can enjoy, becomes only an occasion of jealousy, misunderstanding, and rancor. Empires even have been shaken, or, at least, greatly disturbed by the violent shocks these passions imprint on everything with which they come in contact.

That is the abridgment of our last discourse. To-day I will speak on these three points: (1) the grievousness of this sin; (2) the means of correcting it; and (3) what we must do when exposed to envy and jealousy.

I.

The sin of envy, when consented to in a serious matter, is one of the greatest faults that can be committed. And here, my children, I must be allowed to deplore the illusions which are so common even amongst religious persons. You will scruple at not being a member of some confraternity, at not having said your beads, at not having gone to Communion on a certain day, and yet you never scruple having been gravely wanting in charity through envy, jealousy, and wounded pride. The Holy Ghost says, "With a jealous woman is a scourge of the tongue which communicateth with all."[1] Yes, truly; for just look at that saint-like person who, as St. Francis of Sales would say, seems like an Angel in church; consider her when she returns to her own house, and see how she contrives to dart forth venom on every

[1] Ecclus. xxvi. 9.

one who excites her jealousy. Woe to any one who is an object of mistrust to her, who is even an involuntary obstacle to her love of power! How she strikes and wounds them with the scourge of her tongue! How she secretly lets fly little poisoned darts, which seem to leave no trace in their flight, but which would seriously endanger the moral life of a neighbor, if that life were not independent of those petty intrigues. Then, like the woman mentioned in Scripture, she wipes her lips and says, "I have done no evil."[1] This is a more usual case than you think, and has given rise to the saying of there being so much gall in the minds of religious people. It is a lamentable fact, against which I am forced to protest in the name of the Church, in order that Christian teaching may remain intact amidst the aberrations of man's intellect, and that the world find in them no reasonable grounds for attacking religion.

"Many people," says St. Cyprian, "regard the vice of envy as a trifling fault; but that is a grave mistake, for it is a diabolical sin."[2] St. Augustine gives to the sin of envy an epithet which it is not easy to translate into French, but it signifies cruel, horrible, hideous, enormous; he calls it "a monstrous vice."[3] And he teaches elsewhere, that nothing can be more contrary to charity;[4] that it is a Satanic vice, because the spirit of evil is composed of these

[1] Prov. xxx. 20.

[2] Quoted by St. Augustine, De Bapt. cont. Don. bk. iv. vol. ix. pp. 225, 226.

[3] De ver. Relig. n. 85, vol. i. p. 1253.

[4] De Cat. rud. n. 8. t. vi. p. 457.

two first principles of envy and pride; and that as
the elect form the body of Christ, so the envious
form the body of which the devil is the head;[1] and
that it is the vice which God most condemns.[2] The
holy Doctor concludes thus — "May the Lord preserve the hearts of men, and still more the hearts of
Christian men, from this plague, this scourge, this
diabolical vice."[3]

St. Bonaventure exclaims, with many other holy
Doctors whose words he cites — "Envy, thou inex-
tinguishable fire, thou Satanic imposture, which art
ever pursuing good, seeking to destroy it with thy
pestilential flames, thy guilt is of a deeper dye than
fornication or adultery."[4] "Other failings, though
grave, may be easily cured," says Cassian; "but envy
is like the basilisk spoken of by the Prophet, whose
venom destroys the life of faith and the spirit of
Christianity."[5] "Now the works of the flesh are
manifest," says the Apostle; and amongst these sinful works he enumerates envy, jealousies, and the
vices they beget. "Of the which," he continues, "I
have foretold to you that they who do such things
shall not possess the Kingdom of Heaven — contentions, emulations, dissensions, and envy."[6]

[1] De ver. Relig. n. 26, vol. i. p. 1220; De Virginit. n. 31, vol. vi. p.
599; De Discip. Christ. n. 7, vol. vi. p. 982; Cont. litt. Petil. n. 180,
vol. ix. p. 429; In Psalm cxxxix. n. 8, vol. iv. p. 2215.

[2] De Civit. Dei, bk. xv. ch. vii. p. 614.

[3] De Discip. Christ. n. vii. vol. vi. p. 982. St. Gregory Thaumaturgus calls envy "the poisonous fly of a malignant mind." — In Eccles.
iv. p. 998, edit. Migné.

[4] St. Bonaventure, Pharet. bk. ii. ch. viii. p. 298.

[5] Coll. viii. ch. xvii. p. 1121.

[6] Gal. v. 19-21.

Why such stern words and denunciations, my children? A little reflection will soon make you comprehend the reason. Charity being the first of Christian virtues, it necessarily follows that the worst vices are those which are most repugnant to it. Now envy, and in a certain degree, jealousy, are the passions most directly opposed to charity; opposed to it in their own nature and in their consequences. Envy is annoyed at the good of others; it is this good envy is in pursuit of; and it would willingly see others deprived of it, even though it should not get the good coveted for itself. It may be said that it is God Whom it attacks in its brethren, for it is the Divinity which shines forth in them, since all our qualities, both natural and supernatural, come from God. It is, in one sense, the sin most contrary to charity — it is the sin of Satan. Envy has yet another characteristic, which constitutes it in a special manner a diabolical sin — it rejoices at the misfortunes of others, and rejoices at them even when itself derives no advantage from them. Evil brings happiness to the envious mind; yea, even the evil of a brother; and is not that the special character of the demon's malice? Some one comes to tell the heart of envy that complete failure has been the only result of the enterprises and labors of such or such a one; so much the better, is the answer that rises to the lips! If it does not speak the words aloud, you may still be sure they are uttered fervently in the heart. The envious woman hears that the reputation of one she dislikes is attacked in society, and if not seriously wounded, is at least blemished.

This news to her is like a fresh, balmy breeze passing over the soul, which seems to bring it new life. But all this delight which springs from the misfortunes of others, and this sadness whose origin is the prosperity of our brethren, are they not the two sentiments which bring us nearest in resemblance to the nature of the demons?

Envy has the melancholy talent of so altering the appearance of everything, that what is good is made to seem bad. In this manner the Pharisees asserted that our Saviour wrought miracles through the power of the devil. "Envy," says Peter of Blois, "can embitter honey; wearied of the virtue of others, she maliciously tries to corrupt what is good in them, because she can find no trace of it in herself."[1] What profound insight into human nature! Moralists call envy a serpent, because envy can turn even honey to poison, and the special quality of serpents is to shed into healthy veins the venom they possess themselves. This, too, is a quality of envy. Your neighbor performs some actions inspired by the purest and most generous motives, and his conscience bears him witness in the sight of God that he has acted under the influence of the most sincere disinterestedness. But he had not counted on a little serpent which was secretly playing the spy, hidden in the shade; the wicked reptile shoots his dart, and deposits his malignant venom. With him devotion means self-interest; charity, selfishness; disinterestedness, cupidity; in one word, honey is turned into poison. And what is still worse, he maliciously

---

[1] Epist. xcii. p. 291.

tries to corrupt what is good, because he finds no vestige of it in himself. All this is quite natural: how can you expect that the proud man will believe in love of retirement; or how can you expect that he who knows of nothing beyond the ties of flesh and blood, can understand holy and sublime affection? How can the egotist comprehend the self-devotion inspired by pure charity? Plato says that there must be something luminous in the eye in order to see light; there must be an innate sense of poetry in order to appreciate fine verses; and in the same way, there must be goodness in the heart in order to have faith in it. These are the effects of envy; can there be anything more Satanical?

"Envy has still other tactics," says St. Basil; "for every virtue, having a vice bordering on its limits, into which it may fall through excess, the envious man makes a malicious use of this principle, abusing it to serve his own ends. A firm and courageous person he calls rash and audacious, and the man of reserved character he reproaches with insensibility. He who conforms to the rules of justice is styled cruel, and the prudent man, a rogue.[1]

Envy fastens in a special manner on all merit; the most virtuous men, and the holiest things all serve as a special aggravation to it. "Spanish flies," says Plutarch, "prefer to attack the finest ears of wheat, and the best blown roses; and, in like manner, envy attacks good men, and those most distinguished by fame and virtue."[2] "We may say that every species

---

[1] On Envy, n. 5, vol. iii. p. 382.
[2] On Envy, vol. ii. p. 578. Translation.

of merit is an offence to envy, as every kind of light hurts weak eyes."[1] Look over the lives of great men and of saints, and you will find, my children, that not one amongst them escaped the shafts of envy; and amidst the causes of all the persecutions, more or less great, which they underwent, one of the chief was still envy. "A shadow always accompanies the man walking in the sunshine," says a philosopher; "so he who distinguishes himself above his fellow-men must expect to have envy as his companion on his journey."[2]

Do you begin to perceive, my children, all the heinousness of this vice? And, to complete the picture, listen to the fearful consequences of this deplorable passion. "Envy," says Bossuet, "conceals itself under every possible pretext, and takes pleasure in secret and treacherous schemes. Hinted slanders, calumnies, betrayal, every kind of fraud and deceit, are its work and portion."[3]

I do not, of course, mean to assert that the consequences of envy, carried to so great an excess, are very common. But in little spheres, as in great ones, they are less rare than you think, and envy is one of the chief causes of misunderstandings, hatred, calumnies, and perverse attacks on private life. And besides this, is it necessary that a thing, in order to be gravely reprehensible, should reach its utmost limits? There may be much guilt, yet not the depths of iniquity of the prince of darkness.[4]

---

[1] On Envy, vol. ii. p. 576. Translation.

[2] Pythagoras, Frag. Phil. Græc. n. 59, p. 490, edit. Didot.

[3] Médit. sur l'Evangile, last week, eighth day, pp. 102, 103.

[4] St. Bonaventure, quoting St. Augustine, Pharet. bk. ii. ch. viii. vol. vii. p. 298.

Before envy and jealousy become grave faults, it is, moreover, necessary that we should give consent to them; and I particularly wish to add this explanation, in order to calm unfounded scruples. Some characters are disposed to envy, others are inclined to jealousy. An idea takes possession of the mind, like an access of fever; the blood boils in the veins, but you blush at the feeling, and feel humiliated by it; you resist the temptation, and therefore there is no sin, even although the attack should be prolonged. I will return to this subject, and speak of the means of correcting one's self of that fatal passion.

II.

You must not disguise from yourselves that envy, in characters disposed to that passion, is one of the most difficult sins to be corrected and thoroughly rooted out.[1] It is a moth, the rust of the soul, as I said before, making use of the comparison of the Fathers; but there is no more difficult task than to clear away those little, almost invisible insects from the woollen stuffs where they have taken up their abode. Nevertheless, it is possible to overcome these vices by a series of precautions which experience teaches, and above all by the practice of Christian virtues.

The first and most efficacious means of striving against envy is to put your heart in possession of the true good, by an intimate union with God; by the

---

[1] Cassian, Coll. xviii. ch. xvii. vol. i. p. 1123.

practice of virtue, and the cultivation of that noble sovereignty of soul, which elevates it above the things of this world, teaching it to look on them as changeable, inconstant, and incapable of satisfying the desires of an immortal soul. If the heart be filled with great and holy thoughts; if it hold the rich treasure of divine love, it can never be subjected to envy; for envy, as St. Augustine says, is a sign of poverty.[1] But if the heart be devoid of heavenly gifts, then as it cannot remain empty, it turns exclusively towards the things of this world, falling again and again into the regions of envy, jealousy, and heart-burnings, because earthly goods fill it, but only with a hollow fulness which begets a sickly state of mind, and one of constant suffering. The enjoyment of the things of this world begets envy, because the possessions of one exclude or diminish the possessions of another; whilst the riches of Heaven seem to augment in proportion as they are distributed among a greater number of persons,[2] like those rivers whose sources are abundant and pour themselves forth in flowing sheets of water wherever they meet with a spacious outlet. " When the soul is elevated above the things of this world," says St. Basil, "and the mind's eye is

[1] De vera Relig. n. xxvi. vol. i. p. 1220.

[2] "Abel did not desire to rule over the city which his brother was building; but the cause of his death lay in that diabolical malignity which leads men to envy the good, without any other reason save that these are good, and they themselves wicked. Goodness is not lessened because it is the possession of many; on the contrary, it is greatly increased if those who possess it are united. To wish to be its sole possessor is the way to lose it; and we never have it in more entire perfectness than when we are glad to see others possess it also." — St. Augustine, De Civit. Dei, vol. xv. ch. v.

directed towards the true good, it is no longer exposed to envy, because it no longer believes in the excellence of the treasures of this earth."[1] The second means, which is a consequence of the first, is moderation in our wishes. "Man," says one of the moralists, "would never be envious, if his desires were moderate and in keeping with his character."[2] What are the doctrines of our day on this subject? What are the maxims which influence men's lives? Men are tormented by an immoderate desire of the goods of this world; they seek to grow rich quickly; to make a position for themselves, to obtain high dignities and honors; and are ever dreaming of a step in society above that to which they have obtained. Such is human life as they understand it. This too is the source of envy and interior disquietudes, and the cause of all those jealousies and heart-burnings which render existence one perpetual scene of annoyances. The man whose desires are moderate is always calm, happy, and tranquil; his wishes are few and his enjoyments many. He knows that with confidence in God, and labor in proportion to his position, he will always have enough for his journey through the desert of this life, and that is sufficient for him; he leaves men, like great children, to grow angry and quarrel, and make themselves unhappy about the wretched trifles of this world. For his part, he is satisfied to live with his desires at peace, and having the control of the motions of his own will. The envious man, on the contrary, is always

[2] De Invid. n. v. vol. iii. p. 383.

[3] Alibert, Phys. des Passions, vol. i. p. 339.

uneasy, always agitated by a thousand different passions, like a vessel tossed about on the restless waves; he is eaten up by an internal cancer, and his life, as one of the saints expresses it, is an apprenticeship to the torments of hell.[1]

The third remedy is to nourish a contempt for certain sentiments.[2] Woman is more especially inclined to jealousy by her nature and temperament; for it is better to speak out the truth from a motive of paternal affection, than to disguise it from you. When physicians seek the good of their patients, they lay bare their wounds in order to heal them. But I draw from this fact a very consoling conclusion for your practical guidance; and that is, that the best disposed characters, and the holiest souls, may be subject to attacks of jealousy, and are no more mistresses of them than of an attack of fever. There is no sin in that; sin only exists with consent, and particularly when that consent is followed up with reprehensible acts. Even though a feeling of jealousy should take firm hold of your mind, acting like a veritable blister, if it be displeasing to you, and if

---

[1] St. Zeno. "They are consumed at present before they descend into the eternal flames of hell, and the reason is, because they carry in their bosoms the fires of envy, which can in no wise be carried without burning the bosom of them." — St. Gregory the Great, Super. Cantic. ch. viii. n. viii. p. 542, edit. Migné.

[2] The Holy Scriptures also counsel us to take the precaution of avoiding the society of envious people. "Eat not with an envious man, and desire not his meats" (Prov. xxiii. 6), for there is no poison which more quickly insinuates itself by the contact of words and wishes. — Cornelius à Lapide, in Sap. vi. 25. Therefore the Prophet adds — "Neither will I go with consuming envy; for such a man will not be partaker of wisdom." — Wisdom vi. 25.

you do not comply with its suggestions, you are not guilty, and may even find an occasion of gaining merit before God in this struggle, for it is a trial of your humility and patience. I recollect one day meeting a very good and holy soul who said to me with a supreme effort over herself, " O Father, I feel actually suffocating with jealousy, and the temptation seems to meet me at every turn." The cause of all this jealousy was seeing another soul going forward with simplicity and uprightness in the path of perfection. See here to what lengths this passion's delirium may carry you.

I knew another, a good-hearted person in reality, but extremely eccentric, who assured me that she had at one time experienced a feeling of jealousy of the Blessed Virgin for having been chosen in preference to herself to be the Mother of our Saviour. Of course such extremes are barely credible; but setting aside these monstrous flights of imagination, are there not strange thoughts at work in some brains? What maggots are biting them! Maggots born of jealousy, envy, and wounded vanity. If they were to take visible shapes, so that you could see them all, what a legion of insects would be revealed! What millions of swarms would buzz around us! Now I believe, my children, that in such cases your best plan would be to pay no attention to these freaks of the imagination, nor worry yourselves about such notions, for they only irritate you and destroy your peace of mind. The simplest way is to take no notice of them, to treat them with contempt, and to lay down such involuntary troubles at the foot of the

Cross, where, after a good and fervent prayer, you
will rise again, calm in heart and strong and resolute
of will.

Last of all, my children, permit me to say one
word on a very delicate subject. Should your heart,
as a wife, be wounded in its tenderest part, be prudent, and never give way to quick temper and passionate outbursts, which only increase the evil instead
of remedying it. Employ every means prudence can
suggest; but avoid clamor, contention, and violence.
If you can do so with good effect, remonstrate gently, but remember that anger is a bad counsellor.
Do you know how St. Monica acted in these circumstances, so trying to a woman's heart? "She bore
all this so patiently," writes St. Augustine, "that no
dispute on the subject ever took place between them;
she waited until Thou, in Thy mercy, O Lord, hadst
wrought a change."[1] For she was not deceived in
her expectation, the father of St. Augustine became
a Christian and a good husband.[2] Imitate St. Monica, and peace, a relative peace at all events, will take
up its abode in your dwelling. How many women
who disdained to copy that beautiful model have had
to recall those words of Scripture — "A jealous
woman is the grief and mourning of the heart. With
a jealous woman is a scourge of the tongue which
communicateth with all."[3]

It now remains for me to give some counsel to
those people who are the objects of envy; a class
which includes everyone, for the lowest as well as the

[1] Conf. bk. ix. ch. ix.　　　　　　[2] Ibid.
[3] Ecclus. xxvi. 8, 9.

12

highest positions may excite some jealousy, there being scarcely any condition which cannot look down on one still humbler, and this is all that is requisite to kindle that passion.

St. Francis of Sales highly recommended the practice of this maxim : Do what is right and let men talk as they will. That is the grand rule, the great secret of strength amidst the difficulties of this life. Envy hurts itself only. It is like a poisoned shaft, which returns to bury itself in the jealous heart which sent it forth, infusing discontent and bitterness into its life. If envy pursues you with its darts, imitate that Roman Emperor who, when he heard of the statue raised to him being destroyed, put his hand to his brow and said, "I am not wounded." Do you, in like manner, think that it is your shadow, not yourself, that is hurt. Put your hand to your brow, believe yourself invulnerable, and you will be so. "And," as says St. Bonaventure, "the attacks of envy will only serve to advance your reputation." [1]

These counsels are very necessary, for the atmosphere of this world is filled with narrow, malevolent minds, who, like summer insects, seem to live entirely at the expense of the prey they meet. Franklin wrote thus to one of his friends: "You are certain not to escape the censure of ill-natured critics, who will insult you even while you are doing them a service, like the mosquitoes who attack you in the darkness of night, disturbing your repose, harassing and wounding you, while they are nourishing themselves

[1] Pharet. bk. ii. ch. viii. vol. vii. p. 298.

with your sweat and blood."[1] We must then try to rid ourselves of these insects. Here is a plan I have seen followed at the seaside. The bed is surrounded to a certain height with a frame of wood, over which a mosquito net is stretched. The gauze is open enough to allow of the free circulation of air, but the meshes are sufficiently close to prevent the passage of any insect; and, once established in this aerial fortress, a man can sleep in peace. Let us do the same for our minds. Let us hang mosquito curtains around our lives, and defend ourselves against the stings of those insects. Then, let them buzz away outside, we need no longer disquiet ourselves about their noise. Our mosquito net must be of impenetrable gauze, a tissue formed of two elements combined — confidence in God, and energy of character.

Envy should arouse in us two different feelings: humility, and joy in moderation. Humility leads us to acknowledge the real faults with which envy reproaches us, in order that we may correct them, and though they may be exaggerated, and even sometimes invented, we can thus derive profit from the injustice done to us. The other feeling is that of grave and modest contentment; for envy always attacks goodness and virtue. The bites of some insects prove the excellence of the fruit![2] "I considered all the

[1] Corresp. vol. ii. pp. 138, 139.

[2] "As the sun necessarily brings the shadow, and those who walk in the sunshine are immediately followed by the shadow, thus virtue breeds envy, and jealous rivalry awaits on those who abound in glory. Although envy may bring grief on him who is the object, yet it yields him also solace and joy, . . . for in the same manner as the shadow

labors of men, and I remarked that their industries are exposed to the envy of their neighbor; so in this also there is vanity and fruitless care." [1]

I conclude these instructions on envy with the old French proverb —

> Do good — thy name by envy shall be wounded ;
> Do better — then shall envy be confounded.

increases in the same proportion as the bulk of the body, so envy increases with the growth of virtue. The cause, then, which gives rise to envy — for instance, virtue or glory — also may soothe the grief which envy inflicts." — Cornelius à Lapide, in Eccles. iv. 4.

[1] Eccles. iv. 4.

NINTH DISCOURSE.

RASH JUDGMENTS.

"My brethren, judge not before the time." — 1 COR. iv. 5.

THE faithful of the city of Corinth had been so rash as to pronounce hasty judgments on the Apostle of the Gentiles; he had found false teachers amongst them, who employed all the cunning artifices of jealousy to tarnish the glory of the ambassador of Christ. "My brethren," writes St. Paul to them, "to me it is a very small thing to be judged by you, or by man's day; but neither do I judge my own self. For I am not conscious to myself of anything, yet am I not hereby justified; but He that judgeth me is the Lord. Therefore, judge not before the time; until the Lord come, Who both will bring to light the hidden things of darkness, and will make manifest the counsels of the hearts."[1] John the Baptist came neither eating nor drinking, so austere was his penitential life, and the Jews said, "He hath a devil." Jesus Christ came eating and drinking, leading a simple and ordinary, even a domestic life amongst the children of men, and the Jews said,

[1] 1 Cor. iv. 3-5.

"Behold, a Man that is a glutton and a wine-drinker, a friend of publicans and sinners."[1]

The Wise Man had reason to say there was nothing new under the sun. That which took place in the first ages of Christianity renews itself in the present day. Nothing is commoner than criticising and rash judging the conduct and sentiments of our neighbor. We may make up our minds to this fact — that no one ever has escaped, nor ever can escape, this melancholy law of human nature, even though he resembled St. Paul in the ardor of his zeal, and St. John the Baptist in the rigors of his penance; no, not even though he were a faithful imitator of Him Who was the meekest and humblest of heart amongst the children of men. Do all the good you can, and devote yourself to the exercises of the most disinterested zeal, and you will still be blamed. Imitate the austerity of the holy Precursor, and you will be deemed too severe; be like our Divine Master, full of goodness and sweetness towards every one, leading a simple, ordinary life, and it will be said your idea of sanctity is a very easy-going one. The true Christian will follow the example of St. Paul amidst all these contradictory opinions, and trouble himself very little about the judgments of men, provided that he has nothing to fear from those of God — "To me it is a very small thing to be judged by you."

This question of rash judgments is the most important, most practical, and the gravest that affects Christian morality. Perhaps there is none other

[1] St. Matt. xii. 19.

which so frequently presents itself to our notice, or which causes so many quarrels and misunderstandings in men's lives; for rash judgments are the source of all the words, actions, proceedings, and discord which ruin society. I might add that this is also a matter about which the conscience grossly deceives itself. I am the more desirous to speak on this subject, because it has a natural connection with my discourses on sins of the tongue, — our secret thoughts and judgments being the source whence we derive food for conversation. I will devote two discourses to the discussion of the following points: first, the nature of rash judgments; secondly, their gravity and consequences; thirdly, their causes; and fourthly, the remedies for this evil.

I.

Before entering into the question, it will be necessary to define what is to be understood by rash judgments; for a definition confines an object within its proper limits, and preserves the mind from errors and false interpretations, as well as from those which are only partly true.

Rash judgment is a firm adhesion of the mind to an opinion which we have formed to our neighbor's disadvantage without sufficient grounds. Weigh carefully each of these expressions. In order that there should be rash judgment, there must have been a judgment, properly so called; that is to say, a firm adhesion of the mind, steadily and undoubtingly

enunciated ; as, for example, when one says — Yes, I
believe, and am quite sure, that such a person is
guilty. A judgment must not be confounded with
suspicion and doubt ; they are three shades, or rather
three very notable distinctions, in the operations of
the mind, and in its ascending progress towards certainty or conviction. Judgment is an act of the
mind by which it positively affirms something ; suspicion is a simple disposition which leads us to believe that the thing probably exists, but which hesitates to pronounce a definite opinion ; doubt is, so to
speak, a suspended state of mind, neither inclining
to one side nor the other. I will return later to these
doubts and suspicions. To constitute a rash judgment, the mind must pronounce an opinion in a positive and deliberate manner ; for the thoughts which
present themselves to our minds, and despite our
efforts seem to retain firm hold of our brain and
imagination, pursuing and wearying us, are not rash
judgments, so long as we do not give our consent to
them.

And even this is not enough, — for the judgment
must also have been pronounced without sufficient
grounds.

Charity is no blind virtue, which, under the pretext of perfection, would require us to shut our eyes
to things clearly evident, or very probable. Life
would become an impossibility if, in circumstances
determined by prudence, we were not to be allowed
to judge our brethren ; the wicked might exert their
malice with impunity, the knowledge of mankind
would be impossible, and virtue here below would

resemble an insensible statue without life or motion, a stranger to the usages of life ; or else it would become a fruitful source of mistakes, and the cause of errors and calamities. Do not let us reduce the *rôle* of virtue to this ridiculous position, which no one could accept. It is quite allowable to judge men when wisdom and virtue authorize it; it is quite allowable to know the world, to appreciate it according to its merits, to weigh the wicked in the scales of justice, and esteem them for what they are worth. All the saints have followed these maxims, and united profound knowledge of the human heart, a wholesome appreciation of men, and an intuitive penetration into their motives, with great charity and eminent virtue. The wicked would be, undoubtedly, delighted to have permission to treat the good with injustice, and to force virtue to respect vice, under the pretext that we must not judge our brethren. Neither reason nor faith could accept so singular a code of morals as this, which would turn entirely to the advantage of vice. It is, then, allowable to judge our brethren when we have good and sufficient reasons for so doing ; and by sufficient reasons we are to understand motives capable of influencing the judgment of a grave, prudent man, whose mind and heart are free from prejudices. These reasons may, and ought to, vary according to circumstances and individuals, and good sense should unite with Christian charity to preside over a careful examination of facts, individuals, place, time, and all the other accessories. Such and such motives, which might be sufficient to enable you to form an opinion without

rashness about a person you know, would be quite in-
sufficient in another case. He whose virtue is doubtful has less claim on our consideration than an upright man, whose ideas and conduct are known and
appreciated by all the world. The reasons which
would leave no doubt on the mind of a prudent man
would be sufficient to enable you to pass judgment
with certainty on the first; but the very same reasons
should make you pause and leave intact a man's reputation which has been acquired by a sincerely virtuous course of conduct.

I will make one remark more, which will complete
this definition. A judgment may be false without
being rash, — you may be involuntarily deceived,
and yet have spoken from apparently very good
cause; in such an instance you commit an error, but
not a sin, unless your judgment has been influenced
by some culpable negligence or unjust prejudice.
When these errors are really involuntary in the sense
I have just now mentioned, they are merely a proof
of how fallible the human mind is; but as there is
a risk of their frequent occurrence, you should observe great circumspection in your judgment of
others. Before affirming anything, ask yourself more
than once, Is this a certainty? Am I under the
influence of any unjust prepossession against this
person, — any hallucination of wounded self-love?
Would I wish myself, in a similar occurrence, to be
as severely judged? But I must not anticipate the
different divisions of my subject; so now I turn to
the second question, — the gravity and consequences
of rash judgment.

II.

Is rash judgment in a matter of importance a mortal sin? Yes, most certainly, theologians reply.

"Judge not, that you may not be judged. For with what judgment you judge, you shall be judged; and with what measure you mete, it shall be measured to you again."[1] "But thou, why judgest thou thy brother," says St. Paul; "or thou, why dost thou despise thy brother? For we shall all stand before the judgment-seat of Christ. . . . And every one of us shall render account to God for himself."[2] "Judge not before the time," continues the Apostle, "until the Lord come, Who both will bring to light the hidden things of darkness, and will make manifest the counsels of the hearts."[3] He who judges his neighbor rashly usurps the authority of God; for, to Jesus Christ alone belongs the power of judging the living and the dead. He alone has the necessary knowledge for pronouncing just judgments, or weighing duly and equitably the secrets of consciences, for He alone can search the heart and reins; He alone can reveal the hidden windings of the heart and the secret springs by which it acts. There is often no difference between a saintly and some despicable character, save in the intention which prompts the same actions in both. The one looks up to heaven, the other looks down to the earth; the first is wholly disinterested, and his actions are inspired by the purest devotedness; the second is an ambitious man,

---

[1] St. Matt. vii. 1.   [2] Rom. xiv. 10, 12.
[3] I Cor. iv. 5.

whose chief motive is his own personal aggrandizement. To the public eye, nothing is more deceitful than appearances, nothing more hidden than motives; and the man who, without being enlightened by the light of truth, — without having been placed at that special point of view which alone can give him the power of reading the hearts of men, — slanders his neighbor to himself by rash judgments, exposes himself to the wildest deviations from the path of truth; absolves guilt and condemns innocence; anticipates the day of the Lord, and arrogates to himself a right which does not belong to him, — thus laying himself open to the charge of injustice and falsehood. He makes himself a judge without possessing sufficient knowledge or competent authority; and even were his decisions right, they would still be reproved by God on account of their unwarrantable temerity. "Judge not, and you shall not be judged." And our Saviour also says, "For with the same measure that you shall mete withal, it shall be measured to you again."[1] Ah, my children! these words seriously meditated on may well cause malevolent minds to tremble, who let themselves be influenced by malice in the judgments they form of others! They will be treated at the judgment-seat of God as they, during their lifetime, treated others. They have, perhaps, often besought God to turn away His eyes from their iniquities, and blot out their sins, and not to deal with them according to the greatness of their crimes. They have, perhaps, often cried out with the Prophet, "If Thou, O Lord, wilt mark iniquities, Lord, who

[1] St. Luke vi. 37, 38.

shall abide it?"[1] Listen to the answer. Since you have judged your brethren harshly, you shall be condemned with all the rigor of that Almighty Justice to Whom all is known. Since your eye dwelt sternly on your neighbor, the eye of the Sovereign Judge will penetrate into the most secret folds of your guilty conscience, and cause you to tremble at the sight of your criminal disorders. You who, perhaps, have spent your life in counting every mote in your brother's eye, shall then be shown the enormous beams in your own, which you alone could not see, although all other people were pointing them out to each other with pity. "Judge not, and you shall not be judged."

Besides all this, the reputation of your brethren should be sacred in your eyes, for it is a precious jewel, which no one has the right to deprive another of unjustly. Your brother is entitled to your esteem and consideration so long as he has not forfeited his claim to them, just as you are to his, and they should not be refused without good reason. He, whom you in your own mind hold so lightly, is your brother in Jesus Christ, whom you should love and cherish as yourself. And tell me, you who are so ready to malign the actions of your neighbor,—you whose secret judgments of others are, perhaps, even more severe than your spoken words, — would you not feel justly offended if your brethren, for some slight cause, conceived a bad opinion of you and of your conduct, and treated you with contempt instead of esteem? You shudder, and can with difficulty repress your in-

---

[1] Psalm cxxix. 3.

dignation at the thought. Do not then have two weights and two measures, — one for yourself and one for your neighbor, for charity is one and indivisible.

Rash judgments are also more heinous in the sight of God, because they generally spring from some bad passion. They may disguise themselves under many specious pretences, but, in reality, their root is in the evil passions of the human heart; sometimes in passions so vile and shameful that you scarcely dare avow them to yourselves. If a person innocently wounds your self-love, or vanity, or excites your jealousy, she need expect nothing but injustice at your hands. If she have not sufficiently flattered your pretensions, nor done full justice to some merit, which you yourself are the only one to regard as considerable, you soon find means of revenging yourself in some malicious manner. Hatred blinds you, so that you put a bad construction on the simplest actions, and turn venial imperfections into grievous crimes. Thus you sin doubly, — in the rashly judging your neighbor, and in the motive which dictates it.

This sin is not only grave in itself, but especially so in its consequences. The results, the effects of rash judgments, are incalculable, and ought to terrify us; they sometimes cause fearful devastation in families and society. Look at those two disunited families. Go back to the origin of their quarrel, and you will find it was a hasty, perhaps even a thoroughly unjust, judgment. One of the members of a family had conceived a prejudice against another, without any good reason; for, if we have steam-engines, we have also brains which seem to work by steam, and run away at will with the imagination. This prejudice, in course of time, became a fixed idea. For a long time it was secretly nourished in the depths of the man's own soul, for a long time he had formed grave accusations in his own mind against that individual, and fed the viper with his moody suspicions. It was the offspring of an ungoverned imagination. One day, he let it loose by his calumnies and injurious reports. And hence there are two families set at variance during several generations, and the cause of it all was a hastily conceived opinion, cherished by a malevolent mind.

Why is innocence so often tarnished, so that the most spotless reputations are not safe from the breath of suspicion? Listen to the unfolding of this sad mystery. One of those evil-minded, Satanical creatures, who seem to have received a mission to sow discord, conceives some extraordinary idea in his own brain. His may be a weak mind, or his malice may be the effect of calculation. He breathes his vile whispers into every ear, spreading abroad his own notions, until stainless virtue is blighted and exposed to derision. What was the cause of all this? A rash judgment, the diabolical conception of an evil mind, brought forth into daylight.

I might reduce these general maxims to a fixed rule, for almost every family and social quarrel has had its origin in spiteful tongues, who have always, unfortunately, succeeded in finding listeners for their absurd inventions. Where then are we to look for the source, the birthplace of all slanders and calumnies? In rash judgment. If we exercised due care in judging our neighbor with justice and charity, if we listened to the voices of reason and faith, rather than to the phantoms of credulous and perverted minds, calumny and all unjust reports, so injurious to the fame of our neighbor, would cease to exist, as a poisonous plant perishes when its roots are gone.

I might multiply examples indefinitely; but I shall not do so. I shall stop here, for I have now established the right to draw the conclusion that rash judgments are the first and chief cause of almost all the divisions that disturb the peace of families and of society. And now, do you still dare to question if this be a grievous sin? Ah, my children, the atmosphere of this world is vitiated by the depraved judgments men allow themselves to form about their neighbor; and these judgments, each individually corrupt, are united together, and make up the mire through which we have to wade, — the infected pools wherein the peace of families and of friends is daily lost.

Nevertheless, I will add some explanations for the clearer comprehension of what has been already said: and for this purpose I shall return to some details at which I have slightly glanced as I was unfolding the definition of rash judgment. Theology requires four conditions in order to make it a capital sin: 1. The judgment must be a decidedly rash one; that is, one not founded on really rational grounds. It is not easy to determine precisely what are rational grounds; that must be left to the upright conscience of a thoughtful, God-fearing mind. Generally speaking, when,

due regard being had to circumstances, the reasons
assigned are sufficiently weighty to make an impression on a grave and cautious man, the judgment
cannot be called rash; because truth is not in oppo-
sition to charity, and we are not to call an action
good which is bad. Sometimes the judgment may
be a false one without being rash; thus your neighbor may be innocent of the crime imputed to him,
but appearances and grave external proofs are unfortunately against him, so that there is no rashness in
believing him to be guilty, as long as the testimony
of these witnesses is not impugned. This is what
occurs before the tribunals of earthly justice, where
an innocent man is condemned on account of the
testimony and depositions brought against him; for
men cannot look into the consciences of other men,
and are forced to content themselves with outward
proofs of truth. 2. Rash judgment to be a sin
must be voluntary. Ideas to the disadvantage of our
neighbors often present themselves to our imagination; they resemble so many flashes of lightning
which it would be impossible to arrest. Trying to
fight against them only gives them shape and consistency; our best plan is to take no notice of them.
This advice specially regards those characters and
dispositions which seem to have come into the world
with black crape before their eyes, and who consequently see everything in its gloomiest aspect, and
are therefore naturally inclined to take their neighbor's actions in bad part. The pure white snow looks
gray to them, and the clear bright sky seems covered
with clouds, and they cannot perceive that these

13*

clouds are only in their imaginations, and that they are looking at everything through a foggy atmosphere. The ideas of such people cannot be properly called judgments; they are rather the hallucinations of an ill-organized mind; and as long as the will does not entertain them in a direct and positive manner, they are not sinful, at least not gravely so, even though such harsh thoughts should cling to them with all the tenacity of a nail driven into the brain. But if, unfortunately, such feeble intellects, which are like glasses dimned by the vapor from within, should give way to these inventions of their poor, sickly brains, and let their tongues follow up the lead of their hearts, their serpent-like hisses may cause disorder anywhere.

3. In order that rash judgment should be a grave sin, it must do considerable injury to our neighbor's reputation. The lightness or gravity of the matter must be considered in conjunction with all the circumstances and the characters of the persons concerned; for that which would be a slight injury to some people and in some instances, might be a very serious one in other circumstances, on account of the position and the dignity of the person attacked by the rash judgment.

As to suspicions and doubts, they are not so criminal as rash judgments; and the reasons which lead us to doubt or to suspect others, need not be as weighty or convincing as those on which we found a judgment, properly so called. It may even happen, theologians say, that doubts and suspicions even in grave matters are not mortal sins, because a simple doubt or suspicion does not always inflict a deep wound on our neighbor's reputation. Nevertheless, those cases must be excepted where suspicions and doubts are prompted by malevolence, or where they might, because of their gravity and of the character of the person attacked, seriously attaint his honor.

You have no right, without grave reasons to the contrary, to consider the honesty or good conduct of your neighbor as doubtful, and in many cases this doubt might be of a most offensive character.

What ought we to do when our neighbor's actions are doubtful, that is to say, when they may be taken in good or bad part? The best way of reconciling everything is to leave all to the judgment of God. "Judge not, and you shall not be judged." Still, if you must form a decided opinion yourself, you should lean to mercy, and interpret your neighbor's actions favorably. Such is the rule laid down by St. Augustine.[1] "When an act is many-sided," says St. Francis of Sales, "you must always consider it from its fairest aspect."[2] "If you cannot excuse the action," says St. Bernard, "find an excuse for the intention at least; try to believe there has been ignorance, surprise, or some unlucky chance."[3] These principles of charity are often nearer to the truth than you imagine, and leniency in one's judgments of others is a mark of a superior mind, and of a noble, generous heart, which is well acquainted with human nature, its weakness and infirmities, and only

[1] De Serm. Dom. bk. ii. ch. xviii.
[2] Esprit, part xii. ch. vii.
[3] Serm. xl. in Cant. quoted by Cornelius à Lapide, in Matt. vii. p. 175.

draws from that knowledge a constant leaning to mercy.

However, in practical life and in our relations to mankind, these rules must be read by the light of good sense. Whenever your interests would be compromised, and in every instance where prudent foresight counsels it, you should undoubtedly first observe the rules of charity, but also listen to the voice of wisdom, which will direct you, while avoiding giving any offence to individuals, to act with great circumspection, and take every necessary precaution not to become the dupe of too great confidence in others. You have to receive a total stranger into your house; now it is not permissible for you to form an unfavorable opinion of him without any proof; but you may take the precautions you would do if you had doubts of his honesty; to act otherwise would be imprudence and neglect of your own legitimate interests. When you are drawing up a legal contract with some one, you take every possible precaution, just as if you thought he would infallibly cheat you at some future time; and yet in reality you have no suspicion of his good faith, and it is not so much the person with whom you are arranging matters according to all legal forms you accuse, as the human nature of which he forms a portion.[1]

I think, my children, that the explanations I have given you on this very important and practical subject are in accordance with truth and wisdom on the

[1] For all these questions, see Mayol. de Decalog. Cours complet de Theol. vol. xiv. pp. 866–873 ; Solmantic. Tract de Rest. ch. iv. nn. 87–109, vol. iii. pp. 193–196 ; St. Liguori, bk. iii. nn. 962–964.

one hand, charity and forbearance on the other. Charity must not be confounded with credulity; but it frequently happens that charity brings us nearer to the truth than sterner censures. Strive to find the happy medium, and your little bark will go smoothly on its way, without coming too much in contact with other hearts. Practise charity, united to prudence and a well-ordered life, and you will attain to perfection.

TENTH DISCOURSE.

RASH JUDGMENTS.

CONTINUED.

"But who art thou that judgest thy brother?"— St. James iv. 13.

THE question of rash judgments appeared to me to be the necessary complement to my exhortations on the subject of jealousy and sins of the tongue; and I have, therefore, thought it advisable to speak about this very practical matter, which enters so largely into our daily lives. After having given you a definition of rash judgment, I showed you its grievousness and lamentable results; but while I unfolded the severe principles of theology, which good sense and experience have also sanctioned, I added all the explanations, and admited all the exceptions, which prudence requires, and which prevent the virtuous from being made the dupes and victims of an unreasonable credulity.

To-day there remain three points for me to speak about: the frequency of rash judgments, their cause, and their remedy.

I.

Are rash judgments of frequent occurrence? Have men the habit of judging their brethren rashly and unreasonably? "It makes the majority of men happy," says Silvio Pellico, "when they can believe in evil." [1] "Such is the usual law which guides the judgments of men." [2] It is a sad one, but it unfortunately does exist, and is of continual application. Man, who seems naturally upright and created to believe in God, loves to believe in evil. What did I say, — that it made him happy? Alas! he finds a Satanic pleasure in inclining his mind to believe in evil. Thence comes that vast number of corrupt judgments, which are circulated like so many bad coins, and which the world loves to hear and to repeat, until an indescribable atmosphere of malignity pervades the whole world, and succeeds in injuring the very best-disposed minds. One half of humanity is occupied in passing severe judgments on the other half; and thus each has to go through this assize court in his turn. This does not at all hinder the most courteous bows and blandest politeness whenever they meet. Every man sets up a tribunal within himself, where judges permanently sit, and before whom he continually cites his brethren, in order to have them condemned, without listening to their defence, and often without other witnesses than

[1] Les Devoirs de l'Homme, ch. xxvi.

[2] "The judgments of men," says Cicero, "are, in the greater number of instances, inspired less by truth and the laws of justice, than by hatred, love, desire, anger, grief, joy, hope, fear, errors, and passions." — De Oratore, bk. ii. ch. xlii.

the most unfounded prejudices, or the malevolent
reports of perverted minds. Every passer-by is
seized, apprehended, and if not bodily, at least in
effigy, conducted before this tribunal, and instantly
executed, because he has been condemned beforehand. The absent, too, are dragged before the bar,
and not even allowed to engage an advocate. They
must necessarily be guilty, because they happen
to displease the judge. St. Augustine exclaimed,
" Rash judgments everywhere abound." [1] Yes, rash
judgments intrude themselves everywhere,—families,
society, town and country, are full of them. Each
person possesses a photographic apparatus in his
brain, eyes, and memory, with which those people
who have not the good fortune to please him are
represented under as ill-favored, gloomy, and unat-
tractive an aspect as possible; and when once the
negative has been taken, innumerable copies from
it are disseminated everywhere. "Rash judgments
everywhere abound."

" Fools," says St. Gregory the Great, "always ar-
rogate to themselves the privilege of judging every
one." [2] They give their opinions with so much
arrogance because they are narrow-minded, ridicu-
lously proud, and, as a natural consequence, malevolent. There is a French proverb very applicable
to our subject — " No one criticises the general so
freely as the drummer-boy, nor the learned man as
the brainless fool! " [3] What, indeed, is more com-

---

[1] St. Augustine, Serm. xlvi. bk. xlvi. vol. v. p. 343.

[2] Quoted by St. Bonaventure, Pharet. bk. iii. ch. xxviii. vol. vii. pp.
370, 371.

[3] Le P. Cahier, Quelques six mille Proverbes, p. 123.

mon in this democratic age, when every one asserts his right to talk nonsense, and uses the privilege largely; what is there more common than to hear some wrong-minded individuals set themselves up as leaders in political clubs, talk oracularly, and decide infallibly on men, things, and events, past, present, and future? They would undertake to show a general how to win a battle; an admiral how to manœuvre his fleet; to impart elegance of style to Bossuet, and depth of thought to Pascal. Ah, if they had lived at such an epoch, what a glorious direction they would have given to the course of affairs; if they had only been consulted as to the wisest form of government, what progress humanity would have made! These fools, so infatuated with themselves, excite a smile of pity on the wise man's lips, but, as Boileau says, "A fool will always find a still greater fool to admire him;" so they sometimes succeed in setting afloat notions, both stupid and ridiculous if you will, but what is ridiculous is not always unsuccessful. There is, however, one neighbor that is always spared in these judgments — that neighbor is self. That much-loved neighbor is always made welcome; he is flattered, worshipped, and crowned with a garland of sweet-smelling flowers. He is loaded with compliments which have been craftily extorted, and paid with malicious reservations; and the portrait thus framed is pronounced charming. Ah! if we could only hear what is said behind our backs, and often by the very people who have most flattered us!

We sometimes meet a crooked and perverted

14

nature who sees evil in every one. Such people are like those sick with the jaundice, to whom everything seems yellow. I do not know what kind of funereal crape envelopes their minds and consciences, causing them to see all that is purest and brightest under the gloomiest colors. "When they meet with something clearly and evidently good," says St. Gregory, "they examine closely into it, lest there should be something concealed behind; and endeavor by the most prying researches to find some defects of which to accuse their brethren."[1] "They even go so far," says St. Augustine, "as to give themselves a patent for cleverness,"[2] — melancholy cleverness, which does nothing but grievously wound justice, good sense, and charity. "Charity," says St. Paul, "thinketh no evil."[3] But nowadays we have gone beyond St. Paul, and the world, even that portion of it which calls itself Christian, has set aside the maxim of the Apostle, and replaced it by a habit of hateful suspicion. Nowadays people are ready to believe in everything except in good. Nowadays Christian society is constantly endeavoring to verify the saying of the Italian philosopher, "That the majority of mankind are happy when they can believe in evil." I cannot see that the world has gained much by this singular form of progress. We meet with nothing anywhere but slanders, "evil suspicions,"[4] corrupt judgments, and a malicious, satirical pleasure in them. Men seek to banish the reign of God, which is peace and good

[1] Morale, bk. vi. ch. xxii. vol. i. p. 750.
[2] Epist. cli. n. 4, vol. ii. p. 776.
[3] I Cor. xiii. 5.
[4] I Tim. vi. 4.

will, from the earth, and to replace it by the reign of
bad passions. O world of corruption, of petty intrigues, of base jealousies, thou art punished wherein
thou hast sinned! Thou sowest the wind, and gatherest the whirlwind ; thou sowest evil suspicions, and
gatherest the poisoned sheaves of hatred and dissension. Of what dost thou complain? The husband-
man can say nothing when his land yields him fruit
according to the nature of the seed he has sown.

I now come to another question — What is the
cause of rash judgments?

II.

The first cause is that perversity so common in
this world, and in one sense it is the least unworthy
of an upright mind. The world knows and esteems
itself at its just value: it knows that in the life of
worldlings appearances are often most deceitful when
they look best, and therefore it finds a difficulty in
believing in virtue. But this general reason of the
depravity of the world will not justify a Christian in
tarnishing his neighbor's reputation by suspicions
when he has no good reasons for believing in the
existence of evil. I may think that the world is a
sea of corruption, and I should not be wrong. Still,
I may not extend this conclusion to any individual in
particular without proof. But where the world is
most liable to grave and continual errors is when it
seeks to judge the virtuous, applying to them this
general rule which the corruption of the world has

introduced into a perverted state of society. The world does not know, or rather it malignantly feigns not to know, that in spite of the corruption of the age, there does exist a race of men for whom virtue is not a vain word, but who habitually make justice, goodness, and holiness the rule of their conduct, even although some passing defects, from which no one is exempt, may be pointed out in their lives. But these defects do not by any means authorize us in condemning and tarnishing the whole of an irreproachable life, nor in conceiving evil suspicions of the most virtuous actions. The world does not know, or rather it pretends not to know, that there are some men whose virtue should be untouched by gossip; that, unless from motives of the utmost weight, there is due a greater caution in judging them; and that to such men these words of the Prophet ought to be applied — "Touch not My Anointed, and do no evil to My Prophets."[1]

The second cause of rash judgments is the wicked nature of those who indulge in them. "The vices whose existence we suspect in others are those to which we ourselves are most inclined; and it is the knowledge of our own character which makes us mistrust others."[2] You must have frequently had opportunities in the world of making an observation which throws great light on this truth. The more virtuous a person is, the less inclined you will find him to judge others harshly; the worse a man is, the more disposed he is to judge others with the utmost rigor. The viper's poison lies in itself, and it seeks

---

[1] Psalm civ. 15.   [2] Pensées de Petit-Senn, p. 44.

to project it on all around it. "Men," says St. Augustine, "are more strongly drawn to suspect the existence of those faults in others which they experience in themselves."[1] You know our French Proverb — "They measure every one by their own yard." This proverb expresses a great truth under a vulgar form of speech. If you take virtue as your own standard of measurement, you will not commit the sin of rash judgment against your neighbor; but if injustice, voluptuousness, hatred, avarice, and fraud be the habitual rules of your conduct, your first impulse will be to test your brethren by the same test; and you do not perceive that it is your own conscience you are measuring, and that you are thus giving to all intelligent people a curious insight into what passes in your own mind. "Men," writes Silvio Pellico, "always form suppositions in accordance with the wickedness of their own hearts. Unfaithful interpreters of what is said to them, they give a bad meaning to the simplest conversation and the most innocent acts, and suspect mysteries where none exist."[2] "If they saw a saint," says Father Faber, "they would think him either ambitious, opinionated, or hypocritical. They see plots and conspiracies even in the most impulsive of characters. They cannot judge of character at all. They can only project their own possibilities of sin into others, and imagine that to be their character, which they feel, if grace were withdrawn from them, would be their own."[3] "Such

---

[1] In Psalm cxviii. Serm. xii. n. 4. vol. iv. p. 1866.
[2] Devoirs de l'Homme, ch. xxii. to the end.
[3] Conferences, p. 310.

men," continues St. Augustine, "are audaciously rash in their judgments; they sow discord, entertain suspicion about everything; they do not see with their own eyes, and everywhere spread calumnious reports, in which they scarcely believe themselves. Against such men, what rampart can we raise? Only the testimony of our own conscience." [1]

Depravity of heart is so often the cause of rash judgments, that we might almost lay down the following questions and answers as a general rule: Who are they who are most disposed to suspect hidden motives of pride in the actions of their brethren? Those who are themselves proud. Who are they who are most prompt to fling mud at their neighbor's reputation? Those who are themselves prone to every disorder; whose breast exhales at every breath the odor of vice. Are not misers always ready to accuse their neighbor of stinginess and excessive frugality? And do not rogues always see some cunning artifice in the simplest step; some studied calculation in the most straightforward and disinterested action? "There are some men," says St. Bonaventure, "who can scarcely be got to see good in any one." [2] The reason is quite simple. They see none in themselves, and, as Plato says, there must be something luminous in the eye in order to see the sun.

Another motive for rash judgments is that we seek excuses for our own vices. The wicked man may say what he likes, but he can find neither peace nor any

---

[1] Serm. xlvii. n. 12, p. 364, vol. v.
[2] Sent. Distinct. xliii. vol. ii. art. 3, p. 1078.

available defence against the accusations of his own conscience. Nevertheless, as it is necessary he should have some apparent excuse, some semblance of justification, he seeks for it outside himself, and tries above all to find some defects in the conduct of the good and virtuous that would palliate his own criminal behavior. If, by chance, he does discover some mote in the eye, some flaw in the diamond, he instantly exaggerates and magnifies it, and tries to establish, as a general proposition, that diamonds are of no greater value than the pebbles on the roadside. He would wish to believe himself, and make others believe, in the universal depravity of human nature, in order to be able to say, After all I only do as the ·rest of the world does, and no one is exempt from the same failings. "We believe our brethren guilty," says a moralist, "because we would be glad that they were so; and, therefore, everything which tends to persuade us of it gives us pleasure, and is willingly entertained in our minds."[1] What do I say? There are even persons who seek, by tactics consisting of severe judgments boldly enunciated, not alone to excuse their own faults, but even to hide them from the public. You will meet men and women whose conduct has been, and still is, justly suspected, who affect an extraordinary severity in their judgments of others. A shadow alarms them; to listen to their prudish conversation you would say they were saints. The zeal of the house of the Lord has eaten them up, and if you did not know them thoroughly you might easily be deceived. "People of equivocal reputa-

---

[1] Nicole, Des Jugements Téméraires, ch. i. p. 281.

tion," says M. Nettement, "supply by the implacable severity of their judgments what their conduct leaves to be desired on the score of austerity."[1]   And now we come to the last cause of the malevolence of rash judgments, — jealousy. This serpent, jealousy, which dwells in the brambles along the roadside, and which we sometimes meet at every turning in our path, is also a cause of injustice in our appreciations of others.   "When good is forced on the knowledge of a wicked man," says St. Gregory the Great, "he suffers a species of torture in his inmost heart, and therefore endeavors to dim with the breath of his hateful suspicions the lustre which has dazzled him."[2]

After having thus pointed out the evil and its origin, it remains for me to indicate the remedy.

III.

Let me first make an observation which is justified by reason and experience.   The longer we live, the more daily proofs do we receive that there are often good and prudent reasons for a line of conduct, though appearances may seem doubtful, and even sometimes unfavorable.   There is no one who, in his relations with others, has not had occasion to remark, how near that charity which prevents ill-natured judgments often is to the truth.   We observe this rule inflexibly where we ourselves are

[1] Essay on Serial Stories, vol. i. p. 371.
[2] Morale, bk. vi. ch. xxii.

concerned. We exclaim at the injustice and unreasonableness of those who presume to judge us without knowing our motives, and the very next day, perhaps even the next moment after having given vent to these bitter complaints, we become guilty ourselves of a still greater injustice, and of a still greater want of good sense, with regard to our neighbor. You pronounce judgment with unpardonable rashness on your neighbor. Do you know all the motives of his conduct, and, if you do not know them, how dare you judge him? If men treat you in this manner, you are profoundly indignant. There is a strange contradiction in all this, which God punishes, even on earth, by the law of retaliation. You know from your own experience, that in this world of ignorance and error, the motives of our actions are commonly hidden; and, it is even right, for many wise and prudent reasons, that they should be so. In condemning the conduct of our brethren, we often expose ourselves to the risk of condemning an act of great and sublime virtue. That man whom you hold in such contempt is perhaps a saint, whose whole life is an act of self-devotion in the cause of God and of his neighbor. "There are many lives," says La Rochefoucauld, "which to us may appear absurd, yet for which there may be good and weighty reasons."[1] St. Bonaventure goes still further. He says, "There are many things which we think bad, merely because we do not understand them aright; did we do so, they would appear to us just and reasonable."[2] You

---

[1] Maxims, clxiii. p. 161.
[2] Circ. Regul. S. Francisci, q. 25, vol. v. p. 765.

see, my children, that both good sense and justice
render it an imperative duty for us to be very chary
of unfavorable judgments on our neighbor. At every
wish, every temptation to judge unfavorably of your
neighbor, stop, and first make this reflection — How
do I know but that this action, which seems so ques-
tionable to me, may not have some excellent motive
to justify it? And this proceeding, though so inexplicable to me, may be dictated by the purest charity.
In wishing to pass judgment on my neighbor with
regard to these circumstances, I should be wanting
in good sense as well as in charity, and I should be
doing exactly what I would find intolerable if done to
myself. I should be usurping the right of God, to
Whom alone it belongs, in virtue of His Omniscience,
to know and duly weigh the reasons which justify or
condemn the actions of men. "Always beware,"
said a learned counsellor, "of causes which appear
perfectly clear." [1]

---

[1] St. John Climachus goes so far as to say — "Even though you see
a sinner draw his last breath, you must not condemn him, for you
know not what the judgment of God may be." — Grad. x. p. 847, edit.
Migné. "Men's actions are very difficult to judge," says Father Faber. "Their real character depends in a great measure on the motives which prompt them, and these motives are invisible to us. Appearances are often against what we afterwards discover to have been
deeds of virtue. Moreover, a line of conduct is, in its look at least,
very little like a logical process. It is complicated with all manner of
inconsistencies, and often deformed by what is, in reality, a hidden
consistency. Nobody can judge men but God, and we can hardly obtain a higher or more reverent view of God, than that which represents Him to us as judging men with perfect knowledge, unperplexed
certainty, and undisturbed compassion. Now, kind interpretations
are imitations of the merciful ingenuity of the Creator finding excuses
for His creatures." — Conferences, pp. 25, 26.

You should also be cautious how you believe every flying rumor. Such an immense quantity of smoke rises from the factory chimneys of all large commercial towns, that the whole atmosphere becomes obscured by the dense cloud of vapor spread overhead. In all assemblies of men there are also factories, where lies, calumnies, and malicious reports are fabricated. These, too, ascend and spread in every direction, poisoning with their pestilential vapor weak and badly-disposed minds. Be on your guard against these atmospheric miasmata. Be slow to believe, and where there is any doubt wait before you form a decided opinion. This was the counsel of a Christian philosopher — "Be slow to believe, slower still to judge." [1] Trace a rumor back to its source, and you will discover that Peter repeated what he had heard from Paul, and exaggerated as he did so. You will find out that Paul is a trumpet, and has singularly added to the original sound ; and, in the end, you will learn that there was no truth at all in the report, which had its birth in the laboratory of a bad tongue. Such is the way of the world, and such are the miseries which raise tempests in the lives of individuals and societies. The holy author of the "Imitation" says very wisely, "We must not easily give credit to every word and suggestion, but carefully and leisurely weigh the matter according to God. . . . Perfect men do not easily give credit to every report, because they know man's weakness, which is very prone to evil and very subject to fail in words." [2]

A third remedy is to enter into ourselves, for the

[1] Mars. Ficin, Epist. bk. iv. p. 742.   [2] Bk. i. ch. iv.

purpose of searching into and purifying our own conscience. There we may give free scope to the activity of our minds, pronounce the most severe judgments, lay down decrees, and censure as much as we please. If we take the torch of faith in our hands, we shall find ample matter for criticism and condemnation. "Thou hypocrite," says Jesus Christ, "why seest thou the mote that is in thy brother's eye, and seest not the beam that is in thy own? Cast out first the beam out of thy own eye, and then thou shalt see to cast the mote out of thy brother's eye."[1] It is a fact that men are inclined to judge harshly, by reason of the corruption of their own hearts. They see in others what exists in themselves, or at least they discern every mote in their brother's eye, but they do not see that these motes have become enormous beams in their own. Occupy yourselves solely with your own affairs, my children. Labor to purify your consciences more and more each day, and you will learn to look on your brother with more favorable eyes. You will see him more clearly then, because you will have made clean the windows of your own souls. Here is the advice of St. Augustine, "Endeavor to acquire the virtues in which you believe your brother to be wanting; then you will no longer be sensible of his defects, because they will have ceased to exist in yourself."[2] The same Father says elsewhere, "that charity, while tending to our own perfection, makes us also more ready to believe in the virtuous qualities of others."[3] This is an ex-

---

[1] St. Matt. vii. 3-5.   [2] Enarrat. in Psalm xxx. n. 7, vol. iv. p. 226.
[3] Conf. bk. x. ch. iii. n. 3.

cellent rule, my children, for avoiding rash judgments. Love to shut yourself up in the secret cham-
bers of your own conscience; work will never fail
you there, and you will have no time to think about
others. Try to lead a Christian life, purify your conscience more and more, and you will know how to
appreciate more justly and truly the actions of your
neighbor. Unfortunately, human nature is a tissue
of contradictions; its curiosity concerning the lives
of others is insatiable; but it never occupies itself
in seeking out, and still less in correcting, its own
faults.[1]

Let us also profit by the different counsels the
saints have given us. "Be more ready to believe good
than evil," says St. Augustine. "There is never any
great difficulty in giving credit for goodness, but it
may be a very fatal error to think evil of one who is
a just man and pleasing in the sight of God."[2] Extend this benevolent feeling yet more, for St. Bernard says, "When you see your neighbor commit a
bad action, think that his intention may have been
good, or that he erred through ignorance, or fell
through surprise or weakness. If the action cannot
be excused in any way, then think that the temptation was very great, and that you yourself might
have done the same thing had you been in his
place."[3] Let the evident, known failings of your
neighbor inspire you only with serious reflections on
your own state of mind; nothing will then tend more

[1] Conf. bk. x. ch. ii. n. 2.
[2] Enarrat. in Psalm cxlvii. n. 16, p. 2365.
[3] Serm. xl. in Cant. n. 6.

to your advancement in virtue. Never accuse your brethren with undue severity. A grave, but transient error, sometimes occurs in the life of a good man, whose soul may, notwithstanding, be more pleasing in the eyes of God than those of certain Pharisees, who pride themselves on their stoical strictness. Be very cautious in judging where others are concerned. The goodness or badness of an action generally lies in the intention, and we have not received the gift of scrutinizing the hearts and minds of others, in order to read their motives. Our own hearts are what we know much better, at all events what we can know much better. It is upon that ground we may give free scope to our judgments, and the only fault to be guarded against is over-indulgence on the part of the judge. But, as for our brethren, we should respect their motives, even when the external act may appear blameworthy, and look at things from their fairest aspect, as far as prudence will allow us.

It is of course very evident that, if our moral and material interests are concerned, we may and even often ought to take the strongest precautions. In case we are not obliged to pass judgment on our neighbor, we leave all that to Almighty God. We seek to preserve a possession dear to us, and we protect it against every possible accident which may arise from ignorance, folly, possible or probable malice, and even from misplaced good intentions. Besides this, it is certain that those who have the responsibility of governing others have special duties to fulfil, and that it is lawful, and even in some cases right, for them to suspect the existence of evil, and, without deciding on the degree of culpability, to take prudent measures to protect the sacred interests which have been confided to them.

I shall conclude with a word of counsel and consolation for those who are too much afraid of the judgments of men. I would say to them, whatever you do you cannot escape this persecution, whether it springs from thoughtlessness or malice. Go in any direction, north, south, east, or west; become a hermit or frequent society; be amiable or morose; dress in white, black, or red; adopt in turn the most contradictory opinions, and you will still find people to criticise, judge, and talk sense or nonsense about you. You have only to read the fable of the old man, his son, and the ass. It would be attempting impossibilities to try and cure this evil; we can only resign ourselves and bear our cross courageously. Try to act always for the best, then take no further notice, and let the wave of human criticism die away at your feet. St. Paul exclaimed under similar circumstances — "But to me it is a very little thing to be judged by you, or by man's day." [1] Avoid everything that could give rise to just censure; and as for the rest, you may be in peace. The just soul leaves drones to buzz away outside as much as they will; she shuts herself up in the heavenly hive, and labors to make the honey of virtue. The noise passes away as the wind, but the bee remains enjoying its riches and the fruit of its labors. " To me it is a very little thing to be judged by you, or by man's day."

[1] 1 Cor. iv. 3.

ELEVENTH DISCOURSE.

CHRISTIAN PATIENCE.

"The patient man is better than the valiant." — Prov. xvi. 32.

My intention in these our monthly meetings, which I presume to look on as family gatherings, is to run over, in company with you, all the chief points which regard morality and Christian holiness. I shall not speak of good works only, or rather I shall always speak of them, — for the best work of all, in my opinion, is to do you good, and to bring to perfection the religious feelings which are in you. Let us make a little excursion to-day into a land which lies very near the boundaries of our existence, which forms, indeed, the true foundation of human life, — I mean patience. Every one needs it; it is as necessary to our souls as air is to our lungs. I will devote two instructions to this subject, and speak to-day of the necessity and the advantages of patience.

I.

What is patience? The word is derived from the Latin word *pati*, which signifies to suffer. Patience, then, is a science which teaches us how to suffer. At the age when youthful hopes throw their own bright coloring over everything, when the ingenuous simplicity of inexperience sees brilliant realities everywhere, we often dream of golden days, and of a calm, peaceful, happy life, and accuse the present moment of not granting us all we have dreamed of; and we cast on mankind, more especially on those around us, the imaginary blame of having hindered the accomplishment of our ardent wishes. But as we advance in life, our illusions fade; the green leaves which lured us on in the distance are shrivelled when we come to grasp them, and the soul, grown old before its time, grown old from weariness of the things of this life, exclaims with the Prophet, in bitterness of heart, "Vanity of vanities, and all is vanity." Life is a stage, where the soul which has discovered all that is behind the curtain is overpowered with a feeling of deep melancholy and unconquerable *ennui.* One of the great marvels of Christian piety is its power of teaching man this first of life's sciences, — patience, or the art of suffering. It alone can impart to him the secret, unknown to the world, of keeping his heart green and young in hope, of preserving his thoughts and affections fresh and full of vigor in an atmosphere parched and corrupted by the evil passions of the heart, or the sceptical irony of the understanding. Admirable knowledge, how rare art thou amongst men! And yet it is the true science of Christianity, which every disciple of Jesus Christ ought to know and practise, more or less perfectly. It is the most indispensable, the most necessary, the most in common use of all sciences; and the reason we no longer see amongst us energetic characters as of old, and that the Christians of to-day are mere children, who have none of the manly force of the primitive ages, is because it is wanting amongst us.

This life is a trial, as you already know, my children; it is the time given for the formation of man's character, the moment of his education,—an education which is only begun and completed by means of suffering and contradictions from men and things. The grain of wheat must undergo many changes before it can become the full-eared blade. It falls into the ground, decomposes, and draws a fresh life from its tomb; then rising again, as it grows up it has to bear the cold, the heat, and the fury of the winds, and it is only after it has braved the vicissitudes and the inclemency of the seasons that it attains maturity, and is used to support the temporal life of man, and even then, for that purpose also, it must be ground beneath the millstone. In like manner is it with men, and above all with those who are meant to be of use, and to help in feeding the minds and hearts of others by their own ripe and well-grown thoughts; and who is there who has not to do good, each in his own little sphere, to the souls which surround him; those men who are to be of use must first be thoroughly ripened themselves, and then bruised by the various accidents and contradictions of life. And this ripening of the soul, this forming of the moral character, is only wrought through calm and patience.

Whoever you may be, you have your own griefs and troubles to bear, and you ought to have them; it

is good for you to have them. Do you remember
those young aspirations of mind and of heart, when
at the age of twenty you first entered into the world?
What dreams and projects you had! How many
fairy-like castles in the air! And perhaps many
flatterers and speeches savoring of idolatry! What
has happened since then? Life came with its sad
realities. The men who had seemed most perfect to
you soon· began to look different in your eyes; those
whom you suspected would always cast incense
before you have been the ones to push you most
rudely aside; the soft surroundings, and the couch
where you had hoped to rest softly cradled in down,
all of a sudden bristled with sharp points, and others
seemed to grow on everything you touched, until you
at last entered into yourselves, mourning the bitter
deception, and exclaiming, Is this, then, what we call
life? Yes, that is life, because most providentially
life is a work of suffering, and the wisest man is he
who best understands the science of sorrow.

We sometimes say, "Life is a ship that passeth
through the waves," [1] but we say it without compre-
hending its true meaning. We treat it as a poetical
idea which does not thoroughly penetrate to the
bottom of things. Experience is the light which will
show us how to know the value of expressions which
are sanctioned by use in the language of men. Yes,
life is a ship that passeth through the waves, and that
must in consequence be always agitated; for when all
is apparently tranquil, winds suddenly arise, and he
who is not well acquainted with the ocean is fright-

[1] Wisdom v. 10.

ened, ill, and trembling, while the old sailor looks calmly on, and quietly continues his walk. The human waves which overwhelm our life are, as you know, my children, the people who surround us and the affairs which engage our attention. Every soul, with its own peculiar disposition, its just or ill-founded pretensions; every event of life, with its unforeseen consequences and agitations, is a wave that disturbs the bark of our souls, and even if we succeed in avoiding the first, we shall meet a second and a still more violent wave of affliction. Then, when everything is calm about us, some furious storm rises in our own souls, and our thoughts, desires, and repressed passions are like so many fearful waves, mounting high, and rolling onwards with swift speed, until the heart is sometimes tempted to fall back on itself in a state of utter discouragement.

I do not know the details of your lives, my children, and yet I feel quite sure that with the exception of some slight differences of darker or lighter shading, I have described it in its principal bearings. There are difficulties everywhere throughout man's career, which always surround and buffet him like so many waves; it is useless to hope to escape them: it is only some young being ignorant of life who dreams of a secure position which the sea cannot invade. I might also add that women have to endure more grief and secret anguish in their lives than men. They may meet fewer great shocks than men, because of the less extended arena of their duties; but the pangs they are destined to feel are, perhaps, more acute, because they attack those depths of the heart where feeling is keenest, — perhaps, also, because a woman's heart is more delicately sensitive. It is like one of those exquisite thermometers where the slightest variation in the temperature occasions an instant rise or fall in the quicksilver.

I have often admired the courage of true Christian women, when I have seen them struggling against the never-ceasing troubles of domestic and social life. How much daily agitation occurs in that little lake of home-life which might be so peaceful, — an agitation scarcely visible on the surface, stirring so deeply down below that all seems motionless above! What efforts have to be made to bear the ill-humor of one, and the impatience of another, the susceptibility of some members, and the discontent of others. This may seem a little thing to a superficial mind, or to one who has had no experience of it; but it is enough to stifle every good feeling in a heart condemned to breathe such an atmosphere always, unless it be sustained by Christian motives. And then, when she goes out into the world, what sharply-pointed stones she will meet strewn along her path! Wounded vanity, sharp tongues, and venomous, unappeasable rancors, the outbursts of jealous hearts, and the littleness of narrow minds, ever slow to comprehend any good or generous thought, and ever ready to give you credit for all the whimsical ideas and self-interested views of their own sordid, and sometimes depraved, minds. This is but a hasty sketch of what is unfortunately but too true; if the portrait be not very pleasing, it is because it bears too close a resemblance to the original. And when all this has been gone through, a woman finds she is thrown back on herself, with all the qualities and defects belonging to her nature, with all the aspirations of her heart, with a capricious imagination apt to wander in every direction, with a soul whose feelings are as deep as its desires are energetic, with her will divided between dreams and impossibilities. A woman's most dangerous enemy is often herself. The sharpest blade is the one she holds in her own hand; it is that ardent, impetuous nature of hers which is capable of giving birth to marvels of heroism and holiness, but which may also, badly directed, cause the loss of the vessel and its crew amidst the shoals of the great ocean.

What remedy can we oppose to this great evil? I know but one, patience — the art of suffering, the science of grief. Patience is a power of mind, which, while it feels, can endure, and does not let itself be overcome by pain. An ironclad feels the cannon balls and the oscillations of the waves, but remains unhurt, and continues its onward course through the sea. Patience is the Christian's armor. Send an unarmed soldier into battle, and he must soon fall beneath the enemy's darts; but equip him with sword and shield and casque, as in the days of old, and he will come forth from the combat bearing the palm of victory. And so it is with the Christian. Behold him, like the children of this world, entering the lists of men and things, where he has to engage in as violent and dangerous a combat as on the field of battle. A thousand darts fall on his right hand, as the Prophet says, and ten thousand on his left;

they speed forth from the bow, strike, but fall harm-less at his feet, for he possesses the buckler of patience. It was this that made St. Chrysostom say that the Christian can never be wounded except when he allows it himself, and permits the arrow to enter into the vital parts of his soul. If he puts on his armor, the dart glances aside, falls, and buries itself in the ground. I cannot otherwise explain the lives of saints, very many among whom have led the most troubled existence, full of disturbances and the pro-foundest agitations, anguish, persecution, calumnies, and interior sufferings. All these they have under-gone. And yet they were calm and resigned, they were even happy. "Like," as St. Chrysostom says again, "to a man placed on an elevated mountain, who beholds other men as ants toiling in the valleys below," [1] they remain tranquil and serene, enjoying the light of God.

To understand, relish, and above all to practise these maxims, you must be a Christian, and a Chris-tian to the inmost depths of your being. You must take the things of this world at their true worth, looking at them as so many floating shadows, and attaching no importance to them, except in so far as they relate to God, to the education of the soul, and to the duties of affection and charity. You must become a child of Calvary, — for Calvary is the holy mountain whereon you learn to consider men full of unrest, ever disputing about worldly matters, as so many armies of ants upon the plain. It is on Calvary that the soul steeps itself in the Blood of the

[1] Ad pop. Antioch. Hom. xv. n. iii. vol. ii. p. 183.

Man-God, of Him Whom the Prophet calls "a Man of sorrows, and acquainted with infirmity."[1] Mere human wisdom and the sad lessons of experience may develop stoicism in our hearts, with all its attendant bitterness of feeling and contempt of humanity, but that is the very snare to be most dreaded at the end of our sorrowful journeys. When the soul has been deceived and crushed, it sometimes lapses into harshness and scorn of its fellow-men, and learns to hate while it silently endures. Such is not the teaching of Christian patience; the soul formed in the school of Calvary may suffer, has sometimes had to suffer cruel wrongs, but she forgives. She knows what men are, and maintains a quiet reserve towards those of whose goodness of heart and virtue she does not yet feel thoroughly assured; but this reserve does not arise from suspicion, it is simply the prudent act of a sensible mind, and is always accompanied with great courtesy and kindness. Child of Calvary that she is, she desires to cover the iniquities of all men with the blood of the Saviour; she loves them as her brethren in Jesus Christ, as the children of God, and her patience is blended with many other qualities, which are brought to perfection by being combined together. She is as bronze in her energetic strength, and as oil in the perfumed sweetness of her unction. This comparison of oil is very frequent in the Holy Scriptures; the Spirit of God always presents itself as a symbol of grace, refreshment, unction, and strength, tempered with suavity; and for these reasons it also recalls to

[1] Isaias lxii. 3.

me the influence a Christian woman can exercise. A patient woman is the oil which makes the wheels of life go smoothly, and she is not only patient herself, but she also makes others so by pouring her own sweetness over the springs that give motion to the souls of others. She glides on uninterruptedly, preventing the creaking of the wheels of human life, and serving as a mysterious lamp to light up gloomy and intricate places; like oil she too spreads over the surface of the other more or less bitter liquids which life has to taste of, quieting all things through her almost invisible influence.

How beautiful is this mission of patient women! They take care of, and cultivate, and bring to life again what others destroy and ruin by too great precipitation; and all this without saying or doing anything which men's eyes can take note of. They wait and pray. They wait, but without that irritability and discontent of heart which provokes every one who comes in contact with it. They wait calmly and lovingly with tender forbearance, until by degrees the mountains, that is the difficulties of life, sink down of themselves, the valleys are filled up, and the way made straight. A rash zeal would have spoiled all; a loving patience has kept all. God is patient because He is eternal. Who will give me some of those legions of patient souls, — patient because they see before them the eternity of virtue, and have confidence in the power of truth; who do not rush forward too hastily in the path of good, but who possess the firmness of rocks and the benign softness of a tender charity.

16

I commend this virtue to you, my children, above all others, because I believe it to be the one most necessary for women, who are most exposed to the waves of that inner life which so often upset the heart; also because your moral and physical constitution renders you more accessible to the slightest shocks. With the patience won on Calvary you will be able to calm down all over-vivid impressions from within and without, and be enabled to effect with quiet, almost invisible action, an incalculable good, the more surely that it will be generally hidden from the eyes of men. Patience is indeed a virtue in men, but it is still more the special virtue of women. Woman's heart is daily exposed to the risk of being bruised like the olive; let her, too, suffer herself to be turned into oil, and she will become a perfumed light and unction, and, like it, be the best condiment of all earthly things.

II.

"Patience," says Tertullian, "is woman's chief ornament. . . . Her countenance is calm and peaceful, her brow is serene, no anger contracts it, no cloud darkens it. Her eyebrows are uplifted with joy. . . . The seal of silence reposes on her lips. Her complexion is that of innocence and security. She is seated on the throne of that Spirit of sweetness and benignity Whom no whirlwind disturbs, no cloud obscures, but Who, on the contrary, reveals Himself in His compassionate serenity, ever luminous and calm, such as the Prophet Elias saw Him, under the form of a light and gentle breeze." [1] I shall take this idea for my conclusion, and sum it up, my children, in these words : Christian patience is a source of peace and interior happiness.

One of the ancients took for his maxim, never to be angry about matters, because they could not be aware of his annoyance. The impatient soul is always irritated and in a state of commotion, and yet, let it do as it will, and seek out new ways, it will still always come on sharp, flinty pebbles, which will pierce and wound its bleeding feet. And should it turn aside into country lanes seeking for rest, though there may be no rough stones there, it will meet thorns and brambles, and those prickly plants which botanists call adhering.

All this means that there are troubles and worries always to be met with, both in town and country ; so that the man who chooses to get into a passion has continual opportunities for doing so. There are people whose lives resemble vinegar, in a constant state of ebullition, and who seem to suffer from perpetual irritation of the skin. The soul that is versed in the maxims of the Gospel is well aware of the difficulties of life, she knows that throughout her existence she must often expect to find the stones rough and and the thorns sharp, and takes her precautions accordingly. She clothes herself with stout garments, and puts strong shoes on her feet, and thus defended, walks along tranquilly and unhurt.

Tertullian says elsewhere that a Christian soul should be saturated with the oil of patience. The

[1] Tertullian, De Patient. ch. xv.

observation is true. The man who wants to have everything according to his own liking, runs the risk of losing his peace of mind, and of being always agitated, and like a liquid that has grown sour. His soul is in a state of constant fermentation, and nothing can guarantee such a one's cure, — neither fortune, nor honors, nor pleasure; for the malady of a soul like this is as dangerous as an abscess in the body, which comes not to the surface, but returns again into the body. The true Christian is calm and joyous, because he is patient; he seeks God before all things, and knows that He can never fail him; and strong in this thought he goes through life with the foresight of a prudent man, and the tranquil security of a strong one. He knows that difficulties must come, and when they arise, he finds the advantage of having foreseen them. He does not hope for much from the world, but he tries to do some little good therein, and is patient. Should foul weather increase and foretell a storm, he retires into the interior of his armed fortress, and sleeps in peace, for he trusts in Providence. "He is like a man," says St. Bonaventure, "who has taken refuge in an impregnable citadel, and who, from the summit of the tower looks down with unshaken confidence on the enemy's battalions marching around."[1] This is the true answer to an enigma that has often been an inexplicable mystery to worldlings in the lives of saints, when they saw them, in the midst of saddest preoccupations and important business, remaining as calm as those angelic figures which adorn the interior of

---

[1] De Profess. Relig. bk. ii. ch. xxxvi. vol. xiii. p. 139.

our churches, from whose countenances peace and confidence seem to radiate around. There is nothing to be surprised at; the saints were patient, and had taken up their abode on the immovable Rock of Ages: that is all. I might add, they were not so thin-skinned as we are. Therefore their faces, according to the beautiful words of Tertullian, "were calm and sweet: their brows serene, their eyebrows were uplifted rejoicingly."

St. Chrysostom says that women have sometimes surpassed men in courage.[1] This courage has its source in patience; and woman, though naturally weaker, yet triumphs over man and life's perplexities by means of patience. Learn how to suffer, my children: the occasion so often presents itself! Learn how to suffer; the soul which, like the grape, is crushed, triumphs when it becomes a delicious wine! Learn how to suffer; it will make you strong and happy. Happiness in this world is only found in knowing how to spell each word of that alphabet of human sorrows, which has caused us to shed so many tears! — in collecting together all the letters in order to read and thoroughly understand its mysterious meaning; and the meaning of grief, borne as a Christian should bear it, is peace and love. Peace and love, even in the most arduous duties, as the good monks of the olden time have said — *Pax et amor in arduis.*

[1] De Stud. Præsent. vol. xii. p. 495.

16*

TWELFTH DISCOURSE.

CHRISTIAN PATIENCE.

CONTINUED.

"Be patient towards all men." — THESS. v. 14.

IN my last exhortation to you, my children, I dwelt on the necessity of the virtue of patience, and on its daily uses. Patience is the especial virtue of woman ; for, in consequence of the position she occupies, woman is still more subject than man to the agitation of the interior life, and often finds a cause of permanent suffering in that exquisite sensibility which, while it forms a part of her glory, contributes also to increase her pain.

I have already said, and it is no mere metaphor, but a reality in which she is compelled to acquiesce, that a woman must become as soft as the oil of the olive-tree, for then only will she avoid wounding herself while she succeeds in flowing smoothly over life's wheels and cranks, sinking into and smoothing away all difficulties. But the olive must first be crushed before it can turn into oil. It is not necessary that a woman should seek for grindstones to accomplish this operation ; the stones which grind the

mind and heart are everywhere around her. When
we first enter into life, we are like the shining olive;
but after some years of experience, the olive is no
more — it has been ground down, and only oil remains. This oil is sweet, if patience has presided
over the operation; but bitter, if discontent has found
its way into the mixture.

Patience is, then, necessary for us, and if we practise it we shall obtain strength, peace, and happiness.
"There is nothing can surpass Patience," says St.
Chrysostom. "She is the queen of virtues, and the
foundation of all our good works; a safe harbor,
peace in the midst of war, calm in the tempest, and
a safeguard against all ambushes. She renders the
soul harder than the diamond, and communicates to
it an unshaken confidence through every danger."[1]
A spark falling into the sea does it no harm, but soon
loses its own force and is extinguished; and in like
manner, the most unexpected things may happen to
a patient soul, but they quickly disappear without
having disturbed her serenity.[2]

To-day, my children, I wish to return to this inex-
haustible subject of patience, and enter into some
details which I have merely glanced at before. This
completion of our discourse will not be, perhaps,
without its fruits: she who knows how to suffer has
the key of life.

What ought to be the object of our patience?
And towards whom should we exercise it?

First, towards our brethren, whoever they may be.

[1] Epist. vii. n. 4, vol. iii. p. 707.
[2] In Epist. i ad Cor. Homil. xxxiii. vol. x. p. 349.

Men are full of defects and falsehoods, of injustice
and deceit; and in proportion as we draw up the curtain of the theatre which veils the hypocrisy and the
subterfuges of mankind, we discover things which
make our pulse beat faster, and oppress our heart
until it bleeds with anguish. It is good to know
these things beforehand; it is true it will deprive
the soul of the fresh confidingness of youth and the
frankness of childhood, which willingly flings itself
into the arms of all; but how many false steps and
painful deceptions are spared us by this practical
knowledge of life! It is not enough to know these
melancholy revelations of mankind, we must also oppose to them the rampart of patience, — the shield of
patience. "Leave men to be men," said Fénelon;
"that is to be weak, feeble, changeable, unjust, false,
and proud; let the waters pass on under the bridge;
accustom yourself to unreasonableness and injustice." [1] If you are travelling in hot weather through
marshy plains, you naturally do not count on breathing very pure and wholesome air there; but you knew
and expected that, so you pay no attention to the
fact, or, at the utmost, desire your coachman to drive
a little faster. Accustom yourselves in like manner
to the faults and injustices, even sometimes to the
crimes of men; for men will be men. Will be men
— what is the meaning of that word? Man, deprived
of divine grace, what is he? The Prophet has told
us: "Wretched and miserable, and poor and blind." [2]
The souls which have not been thus rightly prepared
for life's battle, are soon irritated, wearied, and

---

[1] Lettres Spirit. bk. 104, vol. viii. p. 530.   [2] Apoc. iii. 17.

turned sick at heart at every fresh proof of man's injustice; they are strongly tempted to come to the rescue, to crush, and trample, and grind to powder all that seems to them opposed to justice and truth. The experienced Christian does not set himself up as a redresser of wrongs, for he knows that would give him too much to do; he lets the storm pass over, leaving all in the hands of God, and continues his journey. He daily accustoms himself to the unreasonableness and injustice of men, as we habituate ourselves to the winds on the sea-shore, to the burning rays of the sun in summer, and the falling of the leaves in autumn.

And we have not only the faults of others to bear with, but what is still more difficult, the differences in ideas, in taste, and particularly in character. Many people are obliged to live together. God has given to every intelligent being his special appearance, disposition, and manner of looking at things; for as every plant has its own stem, and coloring, and fruit, so every mind has its own shades and varieties. Plants are divided into a number of different families; and we might in like manner classify the different natures, placing those which resemble each other, and have nearly the same manner of seeing and feeling things, in the same category. Minds which are allied in intellect and heart quickly divine one another, and have an instinctive tendency to amalgamate; a word is sometimes sufficient for mutual recognition, — one of those words which opens and illuminates the interior of a soul. And when God is the guiding spirit at these *réunions*, where all are alike

virtuous, there result many marvellous effects, com-
parable even to the harmony of angelic choirs.   God
has bestowed life and benediction on this commerce
of fellow-minds — "For there the Lord hath com-
manded blessing and life for evermore." [1]   Very
often there has only been wanting to a soul this contact with another soul who had these ties of interior
relationship, who was her sister in the divine order
of things.   This is an ideal, you will tell me, but an
ideal, my children, which has been more than once
realized in the lives of saints ; and the doctors of the
Church have written on this spiritual union of souls
words so full of tenderness and poetry, that in order
to understand them perfectly, we should possess an
elevation of character, a heart of gold, and feelings
pure as those of the angels.   I acknowledge those
flowers of the desert are rare ; but still it is necessary
to affirm that they do exist, that they are sweetly perfumed, and that the souls to whom God has made
them known cultivate and guard them with a religious reverence.

I return to the general question : the Creator has
made a great variety in the characters of his creatures.   Each mind has its own form, and style, and
feeling, and language.   There are some passionate
dispositions who see everything in an instant, and
feel everything keenly, while others have all the slow-
ness of the tortoise ; mind, body, thoughts, gait, and
conversation, — all is done by rule and measure with
them.   Some persons are open as the day, frank, sincere, gay, and confiding ; while a little further on

---

[1] Psalm cxxxii. 3.

you will meet self-concentrated, gloomy, and, perhaps, deceitful natures, whose speech seldom trans-
lates truly the thoughts of their hearts. Then,
again, you will find susceptible, jealous, restless characters, as changeable as the clouds of heaven; what
pleases them to-day will sovereignly displease them
to-morrow. You do not know on what side to approach them, for they are all angles and sharp points.
I shall stop here, and leave to you the care of finish-
ing the picture. Behold the world, not the ideal, but
the too real one, in which we have been placed, and
where we must live. These differences of character
and disposition, which may border upon many failings, are often more difficult to bear with than graver
things. There are some almost incredible natural
antipathies. I have met, and you too, I am sure,
with beings who seemed charged with electric currents, and exploded at the slightest contact with each
other. This feeling of repulsion is usually reciprocal; the two thermometers grow heated, and rise to
the same level, and the irritated nerves of the first
arouse a similar irritation in the second.

The Apostle foresaw this difficulty when he said,
"Bear ye one another's burdens." Alas! it is but
too true; we are a burden to each other; and those
that are the heaviest often think themselves the light-
est, and the most wayward dispositions are themselves the most intolerant. Life is not possible unless a compact is entered into between both sides, — a
compact of mutual charity, benevolence, help, and forbearing patience. Quick and ardent temperaments
must, on this earth, bear with the slow and cautious;

and outspoken characters must have some indulgence for reserved ones. Every one requires to have his forgetfulness, his obstinacy, and his susceptibilities overlooked in their turn ; for we — every one of us — give some cause of suffering to others, and what we see occur every day physically, happens to us also morally. When a compact crowd are hurrying along a street, the crowd of people going in opposite directions knock against each other, push angrily with their elbows, and tread on their neighbor's toes. Each one must, then, show some forbearance towards his brethren ; yet it has often been remarked that, by a strange contradiction, the people who are slowest to pardon and excuse the faults of others are precisely those with whom it is most difficult to live, and who, in words and actions, throw mud at every one else. Now, my children, in order to attain to these dispositions of charity, benevolence, and forgiveness, it is necessary to have suffered, to have schooled one's heart to patience, and imbibed the spirit of those words of St. Francis of Sales — " Happy indeed are pliant hearts, for they do not break." Happy the souls who have succeeded, by continual efforts over themselves, in giving to their hearts the suppleness and elasticity of a ductile metal, which does not break under blows from without, but knows how to bend and turn back on itself, and then quietly resume its ordinary shape. This is what our Saviour speaks of when He tells us — " In patience you shall possess your souls." [1] Possess your souls ! Pay attention to that expression, for it

---

[1] St. Luke xxi. 19.

contains a profound truth. The man who allows himself to become irritated loses control over his own soul; it is no longer in his possession, it has escaped from his bonds and gone forth. But with patience you form a circle around your heart, an elastic, pliable band, which does not break, yet resists force from without. How rare are the souls who thus control themselves, and hold the reins of their own mind in a powerful grasp; for the greater number of men let their hearts wander abroad at the mercy of every wind, and every word, and every earthly spleen. Do you, then, my children, be really the proprietors of your own souls; construct a wall around your property, and place in that wall a gate of that well-tempered metal called patience.

But women have to endure more from their own family than from their neighbor, as represented by mankind in general. Woman has a quick eye for seeing many things which escape the notice of a man; and what she does not see she instinctively feels. She possesses a certain delicate appreciation which can penetrate through the most subtle meshes, and find out what is sought to be hidden behind them; hers is that quick divining logic of the heart which discovers more than it can explain, and surprises the thoughts of men in the germ before they are fully developed. A woman requires much prudent and cautious circumspection, not to be the dupe of these faculties, and mistake dreams for realities; for too keen an eye may deceive itself, and too quick a sight may imagine what does not exist, and very often see only their own character reflected in others.

Thus jealous minds will discover jealousy everywhere, and take their own chimerical fears for ascertained facts; and natures accustomed to equivocate
believe that every one else does so too. Great prudence, you see, is necessary in order not to commit
the error of seeing in others the spots that in reality
are dimming the pupil of our own eyes. Besides,
these qualities which we acknowledge that woman
possesses may, if not well directed, contain a hidden
poison. Since the fall of our first parents, each of
our faculties, according as it developes itself, becomes
to us a source of grief and acute pain, unless we
know how to direct its action by religious influence.
Therefore, a woman who is keen-sighted, and sees
through the crooked schemes and meannesses of
hearts, finds in this science a subject of anguish and
tribulation. She sees human nature too clearly; and
it is a misfortune to see things too clearly when one
is not strong enough to bear the consequences of
that sad knowledge. I call it sad, because what is
behind the curtain of human nature is not a beautiful sight, and a rare energy of character is necessary
in order to contemplate it with the calmness and im-
movability of the Wise Man; for we find at the bottom of humanity so much misery, abjection, and
vileness, that we involuntarily recall the words of
Scripture — "In much wisdom there is much indignation; and he that addeth knowledge addeth also
labor." [1]
  Woman, by means of her natural position in the
world, and the quickness of her intellect, is better

[1] Eccles. i. 18.

fitted than others for knowing what passes behind
the scenes on the stage of humanity, and more
especially in the sphere of her own relations, be they
more or less numerous. I do not wish to enter into
any details; but do you, my dear children, make use
at this moment of that faculty which I have just
observed you possess, and divine what I leave unsaid;
or, rather, recall what you know much better than I
do. Run over all the members of your family, from
grand-nephews to those who are nearest to you, and
tell me, What is the result of your recollections?
Do you not find many sad, painful, and even heart-
breaking things under showy appearances? Many
stories of self-love and petty vanities! And oh!
how little that is truthful, sincere, and honest. And
yet a woman must live in the midst of all this. A
Christian woman must live in it, and yet preserve all
her freshness of soul, her virtue, and her respect for
social institutions; she must, above all, never let her
heart wander into deviations from the right path, into
that scorn of men and things, and that discouragement which brings with it the temptation to believe
no longer in honor and virtue. I see but one means
for her to attain to this elevated point and maintain
herself thereat; and that is, patience, which lifts up
the superior part of the soul above the miseries of
life, and allows the wave of humanity to touch, at
the utmost, but the soles of her feet. But who will
bestow this patience on woman? It can only be
obtained through real, sincere piety; not that piety
which is satisfied with exterior forms; but that deep,
innate feeling which penetrates the heart, and

changes its nature while making it divine. He who adheres to God, clinging to Him with every fibre of his being, becomes at last as steadfast as our Lord Himself: "He shall not be moved for ever."[1] Why have so many women of the world withered, dried-up hearts, devoid of faith or trust in anything? Too often because, in their own family, their minds have been undeservedly debased to a lower level, and their affections chilled; while all that was most exquisite in the blossom of a heavenly virginal mind has become faded, decomposed, and cast ignominiously aside. And as those unhappy mortals have not known how to elevate themselves to those regions where the soul cannot be attacked in its own despite, there results those existences of which the actual world is full; those lives of women where the heart no longer gives birth to any noble and grave thoughts.[2]

Patience is also necessary with things and events. Yes, my children, things of themselves form part of our trials, and little things, even more than great ones, were it only through their continual and monotonous recurrence. Let me enter into all these details, for life is composed of details. Who has not sometimes wished to combine events and order them according to his own ideas? Whether they be events of European interest, or little household matters, family affairs, arrangements of material profits, we would have all bend to our will. We would like

---

[1] Psalm cxi. 6.

[2] "Nothing does a woman so much honor as her patience, and nothing does her so little as the same virtue in her husband." — Joubert, vol. i. p. 235. Second edition.

to rule everything, even down to the weather and the seasons; but neither weather nor events pay any heed to our arrangements. The wisest thing to be done is to conform ourselves to circumstances, to do what depends on us for the happy conclusion of an affair, then wait peaceably for its unravelling with as much patience as we can command. Ill-humor will change nothing in the march of events, and has only the one certain result of making ourselves unhappy, and has, indeed, more than once compromised success. Besides this, the events of life are a lottery, at least, as far as human calculations are concerned; we do not know what is really for our good, and often desire what would, were we so unfortunate as to obtain it, become to us sooner or later a source of tribulation and bitter regrets. It is, then, far better, it is a thousand times wiser, to accept things as they come, to submit patiently to them; and in place of trying to bend all to our will, it is both easier and more advisable to bend one's own will to the events of life. Thus the river does not fight with its banks to make them assume another shape; but, on the contrary, accepts the more or less sharply marked windings of its shores, and pours forth its waters tranquilly within them, which does not hinder it from preserving its character as a river, and the quality of its fresh and limpid waters. Why should not the soul imitate the river — preserve its nature, yet make it pliable in its motions and relations with others? Some one has said, — When I cannot have what I like, I try to like what I have.

And must I also tell you, my children, that you

17*

must be patient with God? This expression may seem to you strange; yet I am but translating the words of Holy Writ — "Wait on God with patience," says the Prophet,[1] "and in thy sorrow endure, and in thy humiliation keep patience." Yes, it is necessary, and most useful to wait on God with patience. The sick man is patient under the hand of the physician who cures him; and fine gold must suffer in the crucible of the artificer, who passes it through the furnace to refine and purify it. It is true, God can never cause evil to a soul, for He is the best of fathers, but He often works great good to it under the appearance of a misfortune. He often hides His countenance and veils Himself closely under gloomy clouds while He tries the heart, fathoming it to its inmost depths, and turning the iron in the wound until all the bad, corrupted blood has been drawn out of it. What should be the attitude of the soul who suffers thus, yet retains unshaken confidence in God? She must let the paternal hand of the Lord do what it will with her, kissing it with tender gratitude; she must keep silence, and suffer with resignation; but above all, she must continue to hope and love. And this God, Who thus engages in this trial of love with His children, Who conceals Himself from them only to return to them with redoubled eagerness, Who draws tears in order that He may afterwards console and fill their hearts with happiness, — this God, tender as a mother, will never prolong the trial beyond our strength. He knows the hour and moment for suffering, and the hour and moment for consolation.

[1] Ecclus. ii. 3, 4.

He combines the alternations of light and darkness, heat and cold, for the greater good of the soul, and its more perfect union with its Lord and its God.

Finally, my children, there is one last motive which I have to put before you, for practising patience; and this last subject for its exercise is the most difficult to be avoided, and generally the most importunate of all, for it accompanies you everywhere; it is closer than your very shadow; it is yourself, and this idolized self is not the least of our burdens. "The spirit of man," says the Prophet, "is a leaf agitated by the wind;" or rather, to render more accurately the energetic phraseology of the text, "it is a leaf carried away by the wind."[1] What shall we say of the spirit of woman? The mind of a woman contains many excellent, marvellous qualities, superior in many respects to those of men. I say so, not intending to flatter, but simply because I think it, and I have many times had occasion to utter this truth before in my writings. But beside those supereminent qualities, how many weaknesses, how much impressionability, and how many contradictory impulses do we find? The sensitive plant shrinks back and folds itself up as soon as it is aware, not merely of the touch, but even almost of the movement of the hand towards it. More delicate and more impressionable a thousand times is woman's heart, and scarcely a minute passes that this sensitive flower has not many thrills and starts of every kind, of every degree, and often many quite opposite in their nature at the same moment. Then

---

[1] Job xiii. 25.

there is that heart which desires one thing in the
morning and another in the evening; which is at
high tide to-day and to-morrow resembles the bare
sands; those continual aspirations after the ideal,
and this optimist life amid realities more than pro-
saic. And also that imagination, coloring everything
with its own ever-varying and inconstant shades;
showing us the same object, sometimes black and
sometimes white, according to the sympathies or
antipathies of her own heart; that magnifying glass
which exaggerates everything, and causes us to see
furious monsters where a little grain of sand only is
reposing. What more shall I say? Alas, how many
miseries and imperfections and wretchednesses for
which we are forced to blush! The soul which
studies itself sees itself as a sick man covered with
sores, or at least, as infirm of health, always only in
a state of convalescence, and yet obliged to endure
it patiently.

It is true that we ourselves are the sorest burdens
we have to bear. God allows us to have this knowledge of our own misery in order to form in us the
virtues of humility and patience. It is therefore right
that we should have that which will keep alive within
us the fact of our nothingness; but piety teaches us
to exercise patience on ourselves and our own failings
in the first place. "Have pity on thy own soul," as
the Scripture says.[1] Entertain a tender compassion
towards it, for it has enough of unhappiness to bear.
Treat it not harshly, guide it gently, look at its
wounds with thoughtful love, in order to heal them,

---

[1] Ecclus. xxx. 24.

and never permit it to fall into discouragement. Bear with kindly patience those gusts of the imagination, those wanderings of a fickle mind, those outbursts of the heart, those waverings of the will, — all of which are painful and wearisome, yet very meritorious subjects for exercising patience. Speak to your soul as to a dearly loved neighbor, for our own soul is our nearest neighbor. Break not forth into anger against this leaf carried away by the wind, but help it with gentle and encouraging words, and uphold it with forbearing compassion. If it commit some fault, let us aid it to rise again without any show of discontent, imitating in this the conduct of St. Francis of Sales. This great Saint says, " For my own part, were I to fall into some fault, I would not take myself to task in this manner, exclaiming, Thou oughtest to die of shame, thou blind, imprudent, disloyal traitor ; but would rather seek to correct it compassionately, saying, Alas, poor heart, behold thee fallen into the pit. . . . Ah, rise up again and implore the mercy of God ; . . . take courage, God will help us and we shall yet do well ! "

My children, the English have a habit of taking tea many times a day, and I would advise you with regard to spiritual diet to replace that tea by an infusion of patience, which you can take in different doses, and often in the day. This divine plant is marvellously soothing, and may be applied to every grief and pain of the soul, while it wards off every access of fever. Take at least three infusions a day, at morning, noon, and evening. If that be not sufficient, renew the dose ; this plant can never injure.

With this medical system persevered in during many years, you will, by degrees, form a robust constitution, you will escape spleen, and avoid numerous and enervating feverish attacks of weariness and disgust. You will become calm and firm, tender and energetic, and will arrive at the full comprehension of those words of the Gospel, — "In your patience you shall possess your souls." [1] "And you shall find rest to your souls." [2]

[1] St. Luke xxi. 19.　　　[2] St. Matt. xi. 29.

THIRTEENTH DISCOURSE.

ON GRACE.

"God, Who at sundry times and in divers manners spoke."—
HEB. i. 1.

MAN has great and admirable sides both to his intellectual and moral nature. I have often brought out this truth in my writings no less than in my discourses; and I have done so designedly, for I could never set myself up as an unjust decrier of human nature. But still, to speak the whole truth, and lead no one into error by a guilty flattery, I have also added, what I repeat here, that man is a weak and sickly being. His mind is shrouded in darkness, his will is fickle and inconstant, his body a burden and a temptation. "We are," says the Prophet, "like to a trembling leaf that is carried away with the wind."[1] How simple and how just is this comparison! Do you see yonder leaf lying on the ground? It has fallen from the tree, and has found its resting-place in some lonely spot, without the possibility of ever being able to return to the branch whence it fell. It is next cast upon the highway, where the passers-by may trample

[1] Job xiii. 25.

it under foot, or, perchance, is caught up by a whirlwind, and tossed about to every part of the horizon.
It is a sad, but very true feature of our poor fallen nature ; for we have fallen from the skies, and are now
reposing on the earth in misery and abjection.   Do I
say, reposing ?   Repose would be some consolation in
our misfortunes.   Man, says the Prophet, is a leaf that
is ever in motion ; a leaf that the wind uplifts and violently carries away, and then as violently dashes to
the earth again ; a leaf that is blown about in every
direction, and then falls back to the earth more withered than before.   The comparisons we find in Holy
Scripture are very simple and very vivid, and they
oftentimes present a clearer image than the longest
descriptions would ever be able to depict.   Take a
leaf that has been torn from the parent tree — a leaf
as yet partly green and partly faded ; follow all its
glancing motions, here and there and everywhere, as
it is hurled about by the breeze.   You will read
therein the whole history of human nature, and you
will have a clearer and more distinct notion of it
from such a sight than from the reading of many
moralists.

But happily, my children, God has found out a
means for fixing this leaf of man on its stem, and for
giving back to it all the freshness of young life.
Yea, more, He has given to this leaf of man the
power of reuniting itself to the tree whence it was
shaken off, and of finding, together with life, a species
of immobility upon the parent stock.

It is this truth, my children, that I shall strive to
make you understand in the short instruction I am

going to give you about divine grace. To-day, after
having told you what grace is, and how necessary a
thing it is, I shall begin to explain its many forms
and its varied accents. We will continue the same
subject through a second discourse. The third and
fourth shall be set aside for examining into the necessity of our coöperation with grace, and the qualities
our coöperation should possess.

I.

Grace is an outpouring of the love of God. It is
something of the heart of God which passes even
into us. It is a succor sent to us from Heaven, both
to enlighten and warm ; to rouse us to will and to do
good. Grace, according to the teaching of the Doctors, is a participation of the divine resemblance
which makes us like to God.[1] Grace gives to our
existence a sort of divine form.[2] Grace is the commencement of glory.[3] It is a germ cast into the soil
of the soul, — a divine germ which we have to cultivate in the world, whilst the stalk that springs there-
from should daily increase, till it bursts forth a mag-
nificent, sweet-smelling flower to adorn the altar of
our God. And is not this a truth which is pointed
out to us by the Apostle in the words — " The beginning of his substance." [4]

---

1 "Deiformes constituuntur." — St. Thomas, pt. iii. q. 62, art. 1 ;
De Virtut. q. 1, art. 2, vol. xvi. p. 8.

2 "Esse quoddam divinum animæ confert." — De Virt. ibid. p. 9.

3 2a 2æ, q. 24, art. 3, ad 2m.   4 Heb. iii. 14.

My children, I do not think that there can possibly be a more beautiful teaching than this about the greatness of our destinies. By the outpouring and action of grace on our souls, we are made gods in embryo, and await the day of eternity, when the tree shall be unfolded in all its loveliness.

Our Lord God has so arranged His world, that even in the natural order man is not all-sufficient for himself; and it is with difficulty we can understand how the haughty unbeliever can pretend, in the pride of his studies, that he needs neither revelation, nor grace, nor divine intervention, because he is, as he ought to be, sufficient for himself.

" Man," says Pliny the Elder, "is the only being whom on the day of his birth nature casts on the naked earth, possessing nothing but cries and tears. . . . What a folly, after such a beginning, to believe he has a right to be proud."[1]   " We are filled with shame and pity when we think of the fragility of the origin of the proudest of animals."[2]   May not these wise words of the philosopher be applied to the whole life of man?   During the whole term of his existence, has he not continual need of all sorts of exterior things?   Does not his body want daily food, does not his eye want light, do not his lungs want air?   Does not his understanding cry aloud, unless it would be forever shrouded in darkness; does not his understanding, I say, cry aloud for instruction from teachers?   Has not his heart need of a skilful hand to guide it?   Place a man alone on the earth, without aid or succor from external things, and with-

---

[1] Bk. vii. ch. i.   [2] Bk. vii. ch. v.

out any intelligent creatures by his side, and his physical and moral life will be alike threatened by utter death. And yet the being that is so weak and wretched, unprovided with everything, — the being which nature has cast naked on the naked earth, pretends to be able to do without God, and wants no help from God. He who is so weak in understanding and in heart, he would be sufficient for himself in this divine order, and he would establish himself within the narrow bounds of his own infirmity and impotence! Truly may we say, in the words of Pliny, a man must be mad to be so very proud!

We have need of God, then, in the natural order of things, for it is in Him that we live, and move, and have our being; and if His daily act of conservation did not come to the aid of the act of His creation, every created thing would fall back again into the abyss of nothingness. This is so true, that the Doctors of the Church sometimes call this providential and beneficent action of the Creator — a grace of the natural order.

With still greater reason in the supernatural order, where our nature is radically powerless, there is a still more imperative need of a superior power to raise us up, and impart to us the energy necessary for willing and acting. As the supernatural order is above our nature, it necessarily follows that the seeds of this new life should be shed into our souls from Heaven; and as a something new and divine is created within us, the germs must be brought to us from that higher sphere where they grow. "Without Me, you can do nothing," says Jesus Christ.

Now, this is a speech which fills the proud man with alarm, but is full of charms and delights for the soul which knows and loves God; for it is assured that the Heart of Him Who utters them is every ready to receive it. I fancy I hear a mother saying to her little child, as she opens wide her loving arms, My child, you can do nothing without me, you would only stagger and fall, and I am glad of your helplessness, for it is a kind of loving ruse of mine to force you to keep near to me. The only answer the child gives is to fling itself more deeply and tenderly into its mother's arms.

Grace, my children, is everywhere; everywhere is it hidden : it is the great fluid of souls, if I may so speak, that is shed abroad throughout the whole of immensity; it is like the electric fluid which it is said each being has within his bosom. Grace is everywhere, for grace properly speaking is God Himself, and God is everywhere, and His heart showers down and spreads blessings all around. The learned believe that there are powerful electric currents running rapidly all round the earth, and that they are the cause of many phenomenon which are difficult of explanation. Whatsoever may be the truth of such an hypothesis, the great electric current certainly exists in the order of religious truths. Listen to the Holy Scriptures : "Wisdom goeth about seeking such as are worthy of her, and she showeth herself to them cheerfully in the ways, and meeteth them with all providence." [1] O holy presence of my God, I feel Thee within my breast, in my under-

---

[1] Wisdom vi. 17.

standing, and in my heart, and, as St. Augustine
said, I would rather doubt of my existence than of
the light of Thy truth. I feel Thee all around me;
I see Thee everywhere making signs of love to me;
every creature is a voice with which Thou speakest
to me; and the very stones and rocks and mountains
utter a language that my heart understands when it
is not deafened by the noise of the world. The author of the "Imitation" says, Everything becomes a
mirror of the divine beauty for the just man's soul.
Now, a mirror gives back the image of the object exactly; we may say that the object thus redoubled and
borne on waves of light is perpetuated throughout
the world. And thus it is that the beautiful, august,
and maternal image of God, if I may so speak, is reflected in every created thing, and comes back to us
like the figure of a father and a mother inviting us
to their love.

II.

The grace of God takes every form in order to in-
vite us and do good to us. Let us describe some of
the chief ones.

You must have sometime in your lives, my children, heard a call from God; it is like the noise a
man makes who would awaken us from a deep sleep.
It is evident God then calls us and speaks to us: His
voice echoes in the ears of our souls. This voice
clearly tells us what it is God wants; and it sometimes tells it us so clearly that the soul is appalled at
it, and if it be faithless it flees away that it may hear

no more.   The boy Samuel was sleeping on his couch when a sudden cry was heard, Samuel, Samuel.   The Lord calleth, Samuel![1]   Now this is a mystery which is daily renewed in the world of souls; yea, at each hour of the day, voices sound in the land of spirits, and every soul hears words spoken to it, — words of love, words of sternness, or sometimes words of alarm.   Be they what they may, they are always the words of a father seeking the good of his children.

At other times it is not a voice, it is a motion, an impulse given by an unseen being.   It is a secret power behind us or at our side.   It is viewless, but it longs to carry us along with it.   It is like a friend whom we do not recognize at first, and who at the turning of a street lays hold of us, and out of his love for us wishes to lead us in a way known to him. My children, God has sometimes thus laid hold of you; you must remember such occasions when you were unwilling to go forward, yet when some mysterious being, with loving importunity, urged you on from behind, and led you perhaps whither you would not.   Oh, if you had but recognized the goodness of your God, with what confidence you would have abandoned yourselves to His guidance, with what love you would have yielded yourselves up to His direction.

At other times, again, it is neither a voice nor a motion — it is an allurement.   An allurement is a charm that attracts; it is an indescribable something which another being sends forth to lead us towards itself.   God is a boundless charm; He is a being em-

---

[1] 1 Kings iii. 10.

inently attractive, and if we could but see His beauty, the charm would be irresistible. Here below He has veiled His love, because it is the time of trial; yet still He sometimes suffers faint rays of His divine charms to pierce through the clouds of our existence. And so it comes to pass that our souls thrill with delight when they are touched by the invisible load-stone. There is nothing in the world so gentle, and yet so strong, nothing so resistless, and nothing so sweet in its tyranny, as this interior power. When God, in His infinite mercy, wishes to subdue a soul without offering violence to its liberty, when He wishes to wound divinely with an incurable wound, He almost always acts by way of allurement. He suffers the perfumes of love to escape from the divine essence, and souls in legions rush to His embrace; or He sends from the quiver of His heart one of those arrows that pierce so gently, and yet so effectually, that the wounded soul never recovers, nor would ever wish to recover, when it has once been transfixed. "I will draw them with the cords of Adam, with the bands of love."[1] "We are not drawn to God by chains of iron," says St. Francis of Sales, "but by allurements, delicious enticements, and holy inspirations. . . . Grace is so gracious, and so graciously lays hold of our hearts to draw them onwards, that it spoils in nothing the liberty of our wills."[2] In another place the Saint describes, in his fresh and natural style, the effect which is produced on the soul by the first attraction of grace: "It has sometimes happened that I see a nightingale, awaking

---

[1] Osee xi. 4. [2] Traité de l'amour de Dieu, bk. ii. ch. xii.

with the first dawn of day. It begins to shake, and stretch itself, to unfold its wings, and flutter from bough to bough of the tree whereon it is perched, and then begins to trill its delicious melody."[1]

One of the most ingenious secrets of grace is to accommodate itself to the character and disposition of each one; yea, sometimes to condescend even to our weaknesses; not, indeed, to stamp them with its approval, but to heal them, or, at least, in time to lessen them.   Grace is like a good-natured architect, whom you commission to build a house for you in accordance with a plan which he does not heartily approve.   He resigns himself to his fate in order not to thwart you too rudely.   So it is with grace; it is sometimes content for a time with a defective plan, and it waits in patience for the soul herself to modify it.   Our ways of seeing and feeling here have so many different shades, that we almost fancy grace studies the colors of each one's soul before it enters in, and that the Holy Ghost, like light, possessing in an eminent degree the colors of every mind,[2] loves to put on the tone which is most like our own.   It would seem He can thus accost us more easily, and give us what is most suitable to our wants.   It is, of course, clear that I am not speaking of real defects either of character or of nature.   There is only question of those differences which enter into the general plan of our Creator.   You are of an ardent and lively disposition; grace will also have its ardors, whilst it calms that which is extravagant in your natures. You have a lymphatic temperament; grace will

[1] Traité de l'amour de Dieu, bk. ii. ch. xiii.   [2] Wisdom vii. 23.

slacken its pace for you, whilst, at the same time, it will stimulate your slow delays and the indolence of your progress. You love that which informs your mind ; Grace has her incomparable lights, which, when they are once known and relished, are preferable to all the lights of pure nature. Or, say you are fond of what gives repose to the heart, and all that regards the feelings has an especial charm for you ; grace is before all things love and tenderness, and beneath such a form will love to glide into your heart.

Besides this, every soul, too, has a vulnerable point, some fibre that is very sensitive ; sometimes it has hidden in the most mysterious depths of its sanctuary some invisible point or other which is more unfettered than the point of a magnetic needle. Whoever is master of that point is also master of the whole place. Now when the wisdom of God, Who knows all, and Who is continually making the tour of the world — when, I say, the Wisdom of God in His journeys meets with souls who are worthy of Him, it is at this vulnerable point that He makes His attack, — it is through this secret attraction He will work to draw them to Himself.

Moreover, there are also graces shed upon each one's soul that are nameless, because they are only known by the receiver of them.[1] They come in so impalpable a form, that others cannot distinguish them, nor can the soul that is blessed with them adequately explain them. There are occasions when they become so integral a part of some being or

---

[1] Apoc. ii. 17.

other, that they must forever remain hidden and locked up in the very depths of their soul, and the secret is all their own.[1] " In the kingdom of grace," says Father Faber, " the law which has fewest exceptions is that one according to which supernatural virtues are grafted on natural qualities. Thus, for the greater part, the attraction to devotion is in proportion to the bent of the mind. Indeed, there are souls whose piety is after a poetical fashion." [2]

And here our spiritual mystic enters into a lengthy description of the various tastes of poets : some love scenes of gentle quiet, the tranquillity of the woods, the murmur of brooks, the green grass of the meadows, the village clock, the aged elm-tree, and the laborer returning slowly to his cottage at the close of day. Others, on the contrary, revel in the fogs of the plain, the wild gloom of vast marshes, the silence of deserted cities and untenanted ruins. These love to study and portray in their writings the burning passions of the soul. Those seek the steep rocks, and love to dwell amongst the echoes of the sounding thunder. And so it is in religion. There are many various fields ; each one can choose what pleases him, and follow his own bent, provided only he will take wisdom for his guide, be not exclusive, and never wander beyond the limits of discretion fixed by the Church.

.Oh wonderful charity of my God, Thou art truly in the midst of the generations of men, as a mother in the bosom of her family, filled with an ingenious tenderness for the welfare of her children. Look on

[1] Isaias xxiv. 16.   [2] Bethlehem, p. 253, seq.

that good mother ; she knows well the strong and the weak point of each one, and the advice which should be addressed to one and the warning that should be given to another. She makes herself all to all, and although her love is always and invariably the same, yet the manifestations of it are multiplied. And such, O my God, are Thy dealings with men; Thou givest unto each one the good that suits him, and Thou drawest him by the chord that harmonizes the most readily with his deepest feelings. O Lord my God, I give thanks to Thy Prophet for having told us that it is not possible to fathom all the ingenuity of Thy love. I am happy in my ignorance, for it is a proof that Thou knowest how to love infinitely more than man can understand. "Who hath known His wise counsels." [1]

[1] Ecclus. i. 6.

FOURTEENTH DISCOURSE.

ON GRACE.

CONTINUED.

"As good stewards of the manifold grace of God."—1 St. Peter
iv. 10.

WE may sum up a portion, at least, of our last discourse, in the following comparison. You have a parterre enamelled with flowers, and are vexed to see that it becomes more dried up' every day, because for some months past scarcely any rain has fallen, and you can get no water to water it with. You get up one morning to visit your plants. Every flower seems to have awakened as gay and fresh as yourself; they are all in full flower; their open corallas and their upright stems indicate the presence of a new and abundant spring of life. You are not surprised: a soft and steady rain fell during the evening and previous night, and life has returned to your flowers. But now, consider this wonder well. That rain from the clouds is always the same, yet what different effects it produces. It gives to the lily its beautiful pure white, and restores to the rose the vivid splendor of its brilliant coloring. There is no flower, even

216

to the little violet hidden beneath its leaves, for which it does not prepare the sap it requires. Thus, this beneficent water seems to be metamorphosed while being softly instilled into each plant, becoming alternately red, white, orange, blue, green, and crimson. Grace, the dew of souls, acts in like manner. Grace, too, descends from Heaven, but its action varies according to disposition and character. That man is happy who thoroughly comprehends his own character, and allows himself to become more and more penetrated with the coloring which Heaven has marked out for him.

Light is also a symbol of this truth. Light descends to us from heaven. It is pure and unmixed, yet contains, under an eminently simple form, seven principal colors, which are decomposed according to the nature of the body on which the luminous fluid strikes. Thus, some substances are red, because, on account of the internal molecules, they can only reflect red light. In the same way, grace descends on souls, but it adapts itself so well to the nature of intelligent beings that it leaves different shades wherever it passes. Every soul, like every material object, has its special color, yet the luminous fluid is alike in both, and perfectly pure and single.

We will, then, continue this discourse, and learn how grace makes use of every means to reach us.

I.

You hear a sermon, a spiritual discourse. A sermon is like a copious repast, served up to a great

17

number of guests. Now, it is not necessary at a
grand banquet, it is not even advisable, that each
guest should partake of every dish offered to him; it
would be a certain way to injure his health. In like
manner, it is sufficient, in the spiritual order of
things, if some of the solid and substantial thoughts
of a sermon penetrate into your mind. What am I
saying? There often needs but one, to nourish the
soul most abundantly. You hear a sermon, and at a
certain moment, unknown to other people, nay, which
even the preacher himself is ignorant of, our Lord
pours forth for you, from the lips of him who is in
the pulpit, words of fire, an accent of entreaty, perhaps one only, but it sinks deeply into your heart.
This word is a dart, which penetrates to the lowest
depths of your heart, a choice grace, yea, sometimes
a decisive grace. It is the stroke that God had long
before appointed for your conversion. O happy soul!
bare yet more your breast to receive this divine
stroke to the fullest extent; rejoice and glory in
the wound which lays you low, to restore to you
your true life. It is said that those sailors who go
to fish in the great seas, when they behold a fish
beyond the ordinary size, take a harpoon and hurl it
with all their might. The iron quits the hand, shoots
through the air, inflicts a deep wound, and becomes
fixed, for the weapon is barbed, The wounded ani-
mal struggles and fights against it, but the decisive
blow has been struck. It may sometimes break the
line attached to the dart, and get away, but the spear
remains firmly planted in its flank.

I am convinced that, among the men and women

of the world who affect incredulity, at all events
indifference, there are a great number who have in
their hearts the iron point of a divine lance. They
may conceal it with all their skill, but it does not
the less remain hidden in their inmost soul. I have
sometimes met with men who set themselves up to
fight against God; but, at the hour of death, when
that day of revealing the truth had come, they themselves confessed that this affected fighting with God
was all affectation, and a striving to dull the pain of
that secret wound. I have known men and women
who seemed indifferent on the score of religion, yet
this indifference (and on this point I have received
the most explicit assurances) had been entirely superficial. At the bottom of their souls there had been
all the while pangs, and suffering, and remorse. It is
useless to deny it, my children: there is some one
in all this stronger than man. God is there, and, as
St. Chrysostom says, all mankind united is but as an
army of ants in His sight. Unfortunately, there are
some men who abuse the privilege of free will, and
refuse to yield. They prefer to bear that divine
wound, they prefer to bear that bleeding, open wound
about them, and they try to hide it under bandages
wreathed with flowers, but you may be sure it exists
underneath. "No one," says the Prophet, "can have
peace who resists the grace of God. Who hath resisted Him, and hath had peace?" [1]

I return to my subject. There are some words
which are darts from heaven; and I say, not woe,
but glory and joy to the souls that receive them and

[1] Job ix. 4.

return them again to God. There are words which
sink into the heart, and never again fade from it, because, it is as though God Himself barbs them into
the wound. If you ever receive such arrows, let
them pierce you through and through, and let that
matter freely issue from the wound which is, perhaps,
the consequence of some internal abscess, and you
will rise up again with all the strength and vigor of
one who is perfectly healed. It may not be always
grave offences of which you must thus purify your
heart, but a collection of wretched little vanities, self-
love, self-seeking, a whole troop of too fond attachments, and thoughts contrary to charity. Let the
sharp-edged sword of Providence pierce through all,
and cut away even those fibres which have been
most closely woven round your heart.

At other times it will not be a sermon, but a conversation, which at first appeared of little signifi-
cance. You have had an interview with some truly
religious person, — an interview which a mere chance
seems to have brought about. A word escapes him,
perhaps only a look, which, in the course of the conversation, suddenly gleamed on you with the brilliancy of a flash of lightning, and what happens?
You are not aware of it, neither is he who addresses
you, but a grain of mustard seed has fallen into good
ground, and will send forth vigorous shoots. One
simple word, and so simply said, rests like a weight
divine upon your heart, and that look — you fancy
you are always seeing it — and you are penetrated
through and through by its power. It was the
vehicle of a grace prepared by Providence for your

benefit, and, perhaps, the most efficacious of all your graces. That person has unconsciously been to you one of God's angels, and perhaps the angelic herald of your conversion.

You return one day to your own house, and take up a book. Some sentence in it strikes you, and you cannot free your mind from the influence of that written word. It rises before you, like the ghost in a tragedy. It becomes for you no ordinary phrase, but the special word of God, — a thought which God seems to have put there expressly for you, under the form of those written characters. "Take and read," said a voice to St. Augustine; "take and read." St. Augustine took the book, and was converted. Love to read good books, my children; read those books which speak of God, and of all those things which ennoble the soul. Open them sometimes, nay, open them often; and, when you meet a thought which strikes you and touches your heart, stop there. Meditate on it with loving attention, saying to yourselves, Here is a letter from Heaven for me, — a parent's advice, transmitted to me from the heart of God; it is short and concise, yet I shall find in it all that my heart needs.

The Psalmist says "that God sendeth forth His speech to the earth, and His word runneth swiftly." [1] The thoughts of God are indeed everywhere; they pervade our spiritual atmosphere as snow-flakes fill the sky during the frosty days of winter weather. They fall like invisible seeds, taking root in all well-disposed hearts. Some day, my children, when you

[1] Psalm cxlvii. 15.

are in your room, or walking alone or in public, one
of those flakes of heavenly snow falls gently upon
you; thought descending from above is resting in
your heart, and you feel yourselves clearly, gently,
and brightly enlightened. It may be a choice grace,
— for grace in its outpourings is independent of all
circumstances of time, place, and persons. It breathes
wheresoever it willeth, and sometimes loves to set
aside all the calculations of human foresight. It was
on the public high-road that St. Paul fell to the
ground and was converted.

Another day, grace comes to you on the wings of
prayer and the Sacraments. You are in a church, or
in your own room, pouring forth your whole heart
before God, and, all at once, a soft air fans you, like
those refreshing breezes which are wafted to us from
the sea at eventide; you seem to breathe more freely,
and your whole soul is dilated. This wonderful
effect is also wrought when you receive the Sacraments, and especially the Blessed Eucharist. Then,
not grace alone, but the very fountain of all graces is
in us, abundant and flowing over; we are like a vase
plunged into the sea: we have only one thing to do,
to open our hearts and let the waters enter in.

One of the most frequent forms of grace, but one
under which it is rarely recognized, is the injustice
and malice of men. This may surprise you, nevertheless it is one of the great truths of faith and
reason. "Our enemies," said one of the ancients,
"are often of more use to us than our friends."
Friends often flatter and deceive us, — I mean such
friends as one finds among worldlings, for true

friendship never flatters. Enemies may calumniate
and exaggerate our faults; but, on the other hand, are
there not always some grains of truth scattered
through their falsehoods, — truths which none others
dare to tell us? You have, perhaps, placed entire
confidence in a false friend, and you hear that he has
betrayed you; well, it is a lesson which will teach
you to know mankind better. Is it not wiser to
know the truth than be the sport of perpetual falla-
cies? You have done a good act to another person,
and hear that he speaks unkindly of you in return, —
a thing that often happens, for benefits are a burden
to many. Even your good qualities are turned
against you; any failings you may have are much
more easily forgiven; the wrongs you had done
might be overlooked, but the wrongs of which they
have been guilty in your behalf will never be pardoned you, for such wrongs are the spectres of
wounded self-love, which at bottom knows itself to be
guilty, but refuses to confess it. What always costs
a man most is the avowal of the injustice he has done
to another. Now, my children, I tell you, and I
say so most confidently, that all this is good for you,
nothing more so, when it is permitted by Almighty
God. What! you exclaim; such things good for me!
No; call them rather bad, very bad; and besides,
is not all injustice forbidden by the law of God?
Those who urge this objection are perfectly right; yet
so am I, and in this wise. People who commit injustice towards you are acting wrongly, most wrongly;
they are guilty in the sight of God, and far be it from
me to approve of their wicked deeds. But first, how

often have you erred yourself in the same manner? How many times have you maligned your neighbor unjustly and without proof? I have frequently remarked that the most ill-natured talkers, who gave themselves every license when speaking of others, were also the people to complain the loudest if the most trifling scratch was inflicted on themselves. God often permits that they should meet with as bitter tongues as their own, in order to avenge the cause of their neighbor; it is the law of retribution, which we see every day carried into execution in this world. But even though you could not be reproached with anything of this kind, I still maintain that God makes use of man's injustice for your good, to purify and attach you more and more to Himself, Who is the immovable centre of all things. I maintain that Providence works a marvellous metamorphosis, and without altering the current of events, completely modifies their results. Providence touches the poisoned drink prepared by your enemies with its magical wand, and straightway it becomes a refreshing and cooling beverage. Let, then, Providence take its course, and you will find that "to them that love God, all things work together for good." [1]

The misfortunes of life serve also as a channel for the graces of God. This life is a series of trials, contradictions, and combats, — a battle-field where the fight is ever raging from early morning till night, when it ceases only to recommence next day. This constant warfare is a special favor to us, according to the designs of God, and misfortune is the best and

---

[1] Rom. viii. 28.

ablest of masters; it is a teacher whom nothing can replace, at least altogether, and at particular epochs of our lives. It was this caused a pagan philosopher to say — "There is no one so unfortunate as the man who has never experienced any misfortune."[1] There are some who are steeped in the pleasures of the senses, so full of egotism, so blinded by vanity, and so absorbed in the vortex of this world, that nothing does them any good. They are fascinated with it; they have no feeling or understanding, save for earthly pleasures, and sleep the profound sleep of ignorance about all other matters, especially those that concern religion. God still loves those souls, and therefore He makes use of a last remedy. Misfortune alone can rouse them, and misfortune faithfully fulfils its mission. It enters like a thief in the night, it bursts through all barriers until it reaches that secret, retired spot, where the soul has hidden herself. It strikes that soul, and even with violence, if necessary. It makes her pass through the furnace of affliction; the poor soul would fain fly, but it holds her in an iron grasp until the work of divine grace is accomplished. Do not say this is too hard, too terrible to think of. It may seem so to our mortal eyes; but though, like the surgeon's lancet, it pierces deeply into the flesh, extorting cries of pain from the sufferer, yet the sick man's cure depends on this painful operation. Suffering will be the salvation of that soul; and without it a cure, humanly speaking, would be impossible. Besides this, it is the bad dispositions of the sick man that have made

---

[1] Seneca, De Provid. ch. iii.

the remedy needful. When the tide has ebbed, you may remark on certain flat shores, rocks entirely surrounded and covered with a glutinous sea-weed, until their very form can no longer be descried. Is not this an image of some minds. The thoughts, the desires, the projects of this world, its vanity and sensuality, have gathered so thickly round them, and adhere so closely to every fibre of their hearts, that it is with difficulty we recognize the image of God. What has to be done in order to cleanse those rocks along the sea-shore? Throw them into the great waves, which will fling and toss them about in every direction, and after rounding and polishing them by contact with other rocks, after having stripped them of all foreign matter, will deposit them again, smooth and shining, on the shore. What must be done to tear from some souls the errors to which they cling? The waves of misfortune must buffet and toss them about too, as much as possible. Those hours of your life may be hard and painful to human nature, but the salvation of your soul and its purification depend on them. To that wave which dashes you against the sharp rocks of this world has been given the mission of polishing and perfecting you. And when its work is done, you will render thanks for it, as for a special interposition of Divine Providence. "It is good for me, O Lord, that Thou hast humbled me."[1]

Let me point out, before concluding this discourse, a last form of grace. The soul often feels weary without knowing why. She endures a sort of heavenly

[1] Psalm cxviii. 71.

nostalgia, she suffers from a spiritual nausea, and is ignorant of its cause. This evil is often occasioned by a certain monotonous rolling onwards of human affairs. The soul is stifled, and feels as if it could no longer breathe freely. In this, again, there is a hidden grace, even though it should make it necessary for you to take some bitter, nauseous draught. If the soul drink that potion with the confidence which love of God alone can give, she will be enabled to divest herself of all those ills which cling to our moral nature, and will attain to a more thorough and vigorous state of health.

In our next discourse, I will treat of the necessity and the means of corresponding with grace; that will be the indispensable completion of the two preceding exhortations, in which, after having given you a definition of grace, I showed you how necessary it was, and how varied in its form. The inference to be drawn from these instructions seems to me to be that every human heart can possess, if it so choose, an electric telegraph, whose wires communicate with Heaven. Is not this the meaning of those words of our Divine Saviour, — "I stand at the gate, and knock." Yes, every day and every hour of the day, messages come to us from Heaven; they are of every form, folded in the most various sorts of envelopes, and even sometimes Providence sends us its choicest gifts under addresses which we refuse to acknowledge. Ah, my children, let me entreat of you, as soon as you hear the signal of a heavenly message, go to the place where they knock, and listen attentively. Say with the young Samuel, — "I am here,

Lord, ready to obey Thee." And one day that knock will make itself heard more gently, and a soft voice will say, " Open and prepare to follow me," for God is not now coming to visit you in your dwelling, but is awaiting you in His heavenly kingdom, where He will receive and crown you with His glory and His love. " Behold I stand at the gate, and knock." [1]

[1] Apoc. iii. 20.

FIFTEENTH DISCOURSE.

ON GRACE.

CONTINUED.

"And we helping do exhort you, that you receive not the grace of God in vain." — 2 COR. vi. 1.

GRACE is God communicating Himself to man in order to enlighten and sustain him, to help him to do good, and to prepare him for eternal glory. It is as though a giant were to introduce a portion of his strength into the veins of a child, or rather, it resembles more nearly a mother who shares with her young family all the love and energy of her heart.

Grace is everywhere around us; it is the air we breathe, the light which shines in the firmament, an electric power hidden in the depths of every creature. And as light plays round us with its manifold darting rays, each one more graceful than the other, so does grace take every form, and be found at every turning of the path of life. "Wisdom preacheth abroad." [1] She waits for us everywhere; she speaks to and rouses us, she attracts and conforms herself

---

[1] Prov. i. 20.

to the habits, tastes, and character of each individual. She seems to ask us what are our wishes almost before we have formed them, and practises wiles of love to allure us; in a sermon here, and in an apparently indifferent conversation there; and under some circumstances makes use of the injustice of man in the misfortunes of life, and the inevitable and natural disquiets of a soul created to the image of God, and weary of the world. She follows us at all times and in every place, and may truly say, " I stand at the gate, and knock." " God," says one of the holy Doctors, " is like a mother playing with her child. This beloved mother shows herself, then hides from the child, who runs after and succeeds in reaching her; but she again eludes its grasp until recalled by its tears, when she returns to delight it with her presence." [1]

I will speak to-day of coöperation with grace; a very practical and most important subject, the right understanding of which will reveal to us the secret history of souls.

God could do everything for us without our own coöperation; but that is not His design, and there are several reasons to be given for this arrangement of His providence.

Have you ever reflected on the nature of love and its elementary principles? Love must essentially be free, it must be at full liberty to act and respond. You bestow your affection on some one; if that drop falling from your heart meet only with a hard cold stone, it congeals as it falls. If on the contrary it

---

[1] Rich. de Saint Victor, De Grad. char. ch. ii.

meet an intelligent mind worthy of you, that which you bestow becomes fertilized by the contact. The same thing occurs, and with much greater reason, in our relations to God. Our Lord might bind us to Him with links of iron, as you see a ship laid hold of in the harbor and drawn to the shore. But He will not have it so, because He chooses to respect us and treat us as reasonable beings, whose love should be freely bestowed. He prefers to knock at the door of our hearts, and having knocked, He pauses and waits; if the soul make a movement towards Him, He hastens eagerly to meet her, and if she be faithful in corresponding with His graces, He attracts her heart more forcibly to Himself until she walks firmly forward on the road to Heaven. In so acting, our Lord shows that He wishes us to be, at least in part, the artificers of our own virtue and happiness. He wills that we should have the satisfaction during all eternity of being able to say, This happiness which I now enjoy has been, under Providence, my own work; it has been in part the fruit of my own toil and labors; it has been watered with my tears, and this recollection makes it now sweeter and more precious to me. "By the grace of God, I am what I am." [1] God wishes, then, to do us honor in thus enabling us to coöperate in His work; He "made him honorable in his labors." [2] He desires that the mantle of glory wherewith we shall be clothed in Heaven shall have been woven on earth by our own hands. Do not complain of this, for it denotes a regard for the principles of love, and a desire to render our hap-

[1] 1 Cor. xv. 10.   [2] Wisdom x. 10.

piness more intense, more glorious, and more particularly our own.[1]

"Behold, I stand at the gate, and knock. If any man shall hear My voice, and open to Me the door, I will come in."[2] Note well and reflect on each of these words; God stands constantly without at the door of our hearts. He knocks and waits, for it is a mark of respect not to enter a room without the permission of him who inhabits it. He knocks and then listens, and if the soul says, Come in, our Lord enters and makes a feast of love with her; "I will sup with him, and he with Me."[3] But He sometimes meets souls who will not answer, and others whose doors are shut and strongly barred against Him, and when He persists, they refuse to open to Him. Then God, Who pays far more regard than we do to the laws of love and respect, stands at the door, and waits, renewing from time His request to be allowed to enter. If the soul persevere in its silence or in its refusal, He waits; and will wait, if

---

[1] "The good which we do," says St. Gregory the Great, "originates in God and in ourselves; it originates in God by His preventing grace, and in us by the free acquiescence of our will. If it did not come from God, how could we return Him perpetual acts of thanksgiving? If it did not come also from ourselves, how could we expect a reward? Since, then, we can render thanks to God, it is a proof that He prevents us by His gifts; and, as we may justly expect to be rewarded, it is a proof that we have chosen of our own free will, following the impulses of grace, the good that we ought to have done." — Moral. bk. xxxiii. ch. xxi. vol. ii. p. 699, edit. Migné. "Our salvation," says St. Gregory Nazianzen, "depends on ourselves and on God, and it is right it should be so." — Orat. xxxvii. ch. xiii. p. 299, vol. ii. edit. Migné.

[2] Apoc. iii. 20.   [3] Apoc. iii. 20.

needful, until the hour of death, because love has its
laws which He faithfully observes, and the first law of
love is that the being you wish to love should at least
say, Yes, I consent to be loved.

My children, we are now coming to the explanation
of an enigma which perhaps has often caused us
alarm: the enigma of the conversion or the reproba-
tion of souls, — the reason why so many men live
apart from God, and why others seem abandoned
by Providence. "No," exclaims St. Bonaventure,
"grace is at the call of all men; grace never fails; it
is man who is wanting in his correspondence with
it."[1] I have said that grace is like the ocean; let us
continue the comparison.

Think of souls as of the many prettily decorated
little barks which one sees lying on the sands and
covering the sea-shore during the glorious days of
summer. The tide rises, seeming to woo them, and
call on them to sail forth, while putting at their command its soft, flowing motion. Many of them gladly
accept the pleasant invitation, glide gracefully down,
spread out their sails, and we soon behold them
speeding forth on the great waters. Others remain
behind on the shore: whence that difference? Look
back at the boat, and you will perceive the cords
which hold it fast to the shore, and the iron anchors
still plunged in the deep. There is the explanation
of the mystery. Alas, my children, if we could penetrate into the inmost recesses of a soul, and see all
those secret attachments round which the fibres of
the heart cling; if we could discover all those skil-

[1] 2 Dist. xxviii. art. 1, q. 3, vol. ii. p. 717.

fully-tied knots which paralyze the efforts of grace, we should come to understand thoroughly those words of St. Bonaventure — "It is not grace which fails, but souls which are wanting in their correspondence to grace." Why has such an one no faith, you ask? Why does he not practise his religion? Why is he a bad and wicked man, whilst his neighbor is good and virtuous? You are not aware that for the last ten, twenty, fifty years perhaps, God has been offering His graces to that faithless soul, which still resists His call; and no bird is so skilful in eluding the sportsman's pursuit as the human heart in escaping from God. Our Lord has not abandoned that poor soul; but His work is at a standstill. On the day when that soul at last yields to the ever-constant solicitations of grace, the first onward movement will have been taken. This step will obtain a second grace still more abundant; and if the soul continue to correspond faithfully with it, what then happens is analogous to what I have seen occur at La Rochelle on the occasion of the launch of some great vessel. The ship trembles, creaks loudly, moves forward, first slowly, then faster, till at last it glides swiftly into the waters which are to bear it out to the great sea, while the dancing waves around it are flung back sparkling to the shore.

Will you permit me, my children, to descend into your hearts, and though I do not know all their recesses, perhaps I may still be able to read their histories. Poor human heart! If one has thoroughly studied its working in some characters, one can know almost every detail of their life's romance, and can foretell the adventures which will everywhere befall them. I shall now take up again the description of the forms of grace, such as I have laid them down in the preceding instructions.

God stands at the gate, and knocks, the Scriptures tell us. How many times has He not knocked at the door of your heart? Have you answered Him? Perhaps He is knocking there at this very moment. Be silent and listen. Yes, it is certainly He Who knocks, for friends knock in a manner which we cannot fail to recognize. God more especially has His own particular way of knocking, which none other can counterfeit. But you do not wish to hear Him, and so you do what, perhaps, you have often done, when, having shut the door of your own room, you turned the key to escape some inopportune visitor. You let him stand at the door, and said — There, let him knock now as long as he likes. Or you tried to deceive yourself, and, making a noise in the room, you said, Nobody has been knocking: it was merely some sound outside, or, perhaps, I only dreamt it. Faithless soul, cherish no such illusions: it is God Himself Who knocks, and you will have no rest till you open to Him. I fancy I hear you say now, Ah! it is God Who is there: well, let Him come in. But this is merely a new ruse on your part, for you conduct Him to the room set aside for the reception of strangers and mere acquaintances, where the trivialities only of life are treated, and the conversation turns on rain and fine weather. It is here you desire to have our Lord remain, because you fear beyond everything that He wishes to speak with you about the inmost secrets of

your heart. But though you may deceive men, you
cannot deceive God. It is not in that grand recep-
tion-room He will remain, but He intends to penetrate into the most hidden chamber of your heart;
into that corner you know of, that mysterious, secret
corner, where you scarcely allow daylight to enter.
You are so afraid any one should see clearly therein.
Yes, it is there, past all those ante-chambers, through
all those hangings of tapestry, that God wishes to
speak to you. "Behold, I stand at the gate, and
knock."   Alas! no; the door of that room is kept
closed, fastened with bolt and bar, and you will not
allow Him to come there. You even sometimes
specially exclude God, for you fear His eye above all
others. He would see too much, and would give you
counsels which you are resolved beforehand not to
follow. I can quite understand now why you take
all these precautions against Him.

We have just seen that our Lord knocks at the
door of the soul. Another form of grace is appeal.
Yes, God calls, and you hear Him distinctly. His
voice is clear and true, and what He says is distinctly
expressed. God must certainly have thus spoken
sometimes to you also, my children, for He never
ceases for a single instant, says St. Augustine, to
speak to all rational beings, and makes Himself particularly heard by souls whom He loves so tenderly
as He does yours. You have, then, heard that paternal voice; you have heard it, perhaps, oftener than
you wished to do; but have you not acted as the
child does when its mother comes to call it in the
morning? It hides itself in its bed, pretends not to

hear, or only half answers; then when its mother returns after the lapse of an hour, and finds it still in the same place, it endeavors to stammer out some excuse. I am only now commenting on a sentence from Holy Writ — "I called," says the Lord, "and you refused." [1] Or you did as Adam and Eve did when they heard the voice of God — "I heard Thy voice in the garden, and I was afraid." [2] You, too, have perhaps sinned like Adam and Eve, concealing yourselves when you heard God speaking. But all that is useless; God will walk in your garden, and pursue you everywhere, — in society and in solitude. You may escape from hearing the voice of a man who importunes you; you may avoid his house, and never let him enter yours; but the voice of God sounds wheresoever and whensoever it willeth, and it need not ask for permission to enter, for every place is His. It throws down the cedars of Lebanon, says the Prophet: that is to say, it is so strong, nothing can stand against it; it makes itself heard through the roaring of the waves: that is to say, it subdues and imposes silence on all earthly passions when it so chooses. "The voice of the Lord breaketh the cedars. The voice of the Lord is upon the waters." [3] That all-powerful voice will call you, saying as it did to our first parent, "Where art thou, Adam?" I entreat of you not to answer as Adam did, but follow rather the counsel of St. Augustine, and if you have something grave wherewith to reproach yourself, to escape the justice of God by flinging yourself into the arms of His mercy. Say with the prodigal,

---

[1] Prov. i. 24.   [2] Gen. iii. 10.   [3] Psalm xxviii.

"Father, I have sinned against Heaven, and before Thee." These few simple words will disarm justice, and you will meet only the outstretched arms of a Father, and, even if you desire it, the still tenderer embrace of a mother, for God is everything to the soul, everything that she wishes Him to be. *Quid quid volueris*, says St. Chrysostom.[1]

I have spoken of grace as being at times a movement; a symbolical expression which is full of truth. God sometimes forces us on, and an invisible hand seems to impel us forward. Recall some certain events in your life. Did not God then urge you to go forward? Did you not feel the pressure of His hand, and experience an involuntary motion through your whole being? If you are beside the sea-shore, or on a mountain, in tempestuous weather, you feel the wind impel you on in one direction, in spite of yourself; and if you want to go against, it you must make great efforts to resist its force. Grace, too, has its violent gusts. "And suddenly there came a sound from Heaven," says Holy Writ, "as of a mighty wind coming."[2] Now there are three ways of escaping the force of the wind: to face it boldly, to avoid it, or to seek a shelter against its violence. Is not this what you have done? You have, perhaps, hardened yourself in an obstinate resistance to grace, and have sought to fight against and openly withstand the divine impelling power, — though I believe such instances are rare. Then you have found another way of escaping from God, slipping aside, as it were, and letting Him pass by; or you have

---

[1] In Matt. Hom. lxxvi. vol. vii. p. 833. [2] Acts ii. 2.

sought shelter against Him, erecting ramparts for your protection, such as men's passions well know how to raise, and behind which they believe themselves to be safe.

The most irresistible form of grace is attraction; that is to say, an emanation from the heart of God, —an emanation full of love, which takes our hearts by their most susceptible side, and subjugates them by pouring new life into them. After a fervent Communion, during one of those moments of the cause of whose coming and going we are ignorant, have you not felt that God was nearer to you, that He was drawing you to Himself, folding you to His heart, and cradling you in the softest slumbers? Even after faults committed, have you not sometimes felt that sweet attraction of our good and merciful God? I think that one of the greatest faults into which we can fall, my children, is resisting the grace of God when He thus seeks to allure us with the sweet odors of His love. Judas's greatest crime, according to the idea of St. Leo, was, not having denied his Master, but having resisted the call of that loving word, Friend. There are days when it seems to us as though God more particularly desired to do us good; when, as St. John of the Cross says, He opens His heart, and we see renewed in the world of souls what happens to flowers in the spring-time; when the blossoms in the parterres expand, the air is balmy with sweet scents, and everything seems to have life. To resist God in such moments is, I repeat again, one of the greatest faults that can be committed. You shall judge of this by your own feelings. You have a child whom you love with the utmost tenderness; yet there are moments in the lives of mothers when, through some mysterious law of love, they feel a need of showing still greater affection. If the heart of your child be as fervent to receive in that hour of blessing as yours is to give, then fresh mysteries of tenderness and love will reveal themselves to both. If, on the contrary, its heart be cold and insensible; if it seem to have no comprehension of your meaning; an icy reaction is quickly wrought in you, which spreads to all the lesser degrees of your heart's thermometer. Love is so constituted, that if it be not understood at the moment it seeks to make itself known, it falls back on itself, and may even turn into a glacier. I must, however, add that God does not resemble His creatures in this point, for we can always rekindle and revive the fire of love in Him.

I shall continue, my children, to trace the different forms of grace which I enumerated in my last instructions, as I wish to make a little practical observation for your benefit on each of them. You have been listening to a sermon, or to some pious conversation. Some words of it, one idea in particular, has remained in your memory and fixed itself more deeply in your heart than you desired; it has thrown light on things you did not know before, or rather which you did not wish to know. For some ideas are like bombs, which fall, then burst, scattering their fragments all around, demolishing the work of men, and all those castles in the air which some imaginations love to erect for themselves. Everything is thrown to the ground in an instant and utterly de-

stroyed; no hope of reviving them — a shell has
passed there. Fortunate disaster! Poor soul, so
dear to God that He wills to save it in spite of itself!
You do not see that it is God Who pointed that gun
and directed the explosion of the shell. The ar-
tillery-man knows nothing of the ravages he has
caused; he is not in the least aware that your city is
now in flames. Yes, you are now on fire; and so
much the better, for there were many old houses in
the city of your heart, many useless ruins, perhaps,
and behind each of those tottering walls whole heaps
of rubbish, and of things which it is as well not to
speak of. But we will not recall what grace has
burnt away and purified. So much the better for
you that your town has been burnt down. Almighty
God will rebuild you a far more beautiful and magnif-
icent city, if you will lend your aid to the work, and
not hinder what He wishes to do. "And I saw the
holy city, the new Jerusalem."[1]

At other times grace hides itself in the speech of
a friend, or it may be in a glance, which seems nothing, yet is everything. It is God Who manifests
Himself to you in that glance from His creatures;
and why should it not be so? "He is abroad on the
wings of the wind," says the Prophet. It was God
who spoke to you, when He made your friend's heart
His interpreter; it was He Who caused those words
of enlightenment to flow from his lips. He lit that
glance of subtle flame, and mingled an elixir of precious graces in those words; for speech, says St.
Augustine, "is the vase which contains the thoughts

of men." I entreat you not to let that heavenly perfume escape; carry it away in a closely sealed vase,
for the happy future of your soul may lie in that
sweet-smelling *flaçon.*

It is possible and more than probable that you
have enemies, for every one has them more or less.
You will, perhaps, have many merely because you
have done some good; for there are people to whom
gratitude is a weighty burden, and they seek pretexts
and get up apparent reasons for enmity, merely to get
rid of it. For this cause only you will have enemies,
and I have already told you how useful you may
make them. The defects of each person form a
plaster[1] for his neighbor, according to the idea of
one of the saints; I am translating the text literally.
But one's enemies are the best and most healing
plasters in some disorders, although I cannot call
them anodynes. You have a tumor in your head or
on your legs. No, I mistake; it is your mind or your
heart that is affected, and you go to seek a cure in
the medicine-chest of a friend. You are wrong; you
would have only found some temporary alleviation of
your pain there; and Providence, the best of all doctors, has charged some one not exactly a friend to
prepare a mustard blister for you in the very best
manner. That is an infallible specific; one hour's
application of it and you are cured. What I am now
saying, my children, is really of grave importance,
for our enemies, if turned to a right use, may be
of the utmost advantage to us without their own

[1] "Cataplasma." St. John Climachus, Liber ad pastorem, ch. ii.
p. 1170, edit. Migné.

knowledge and against their own wishes, as medicine finds its most efficacious remedies in active poisons when they are properly administered.

But you have a still more dangerous enemy in yourself, in your own self-deceiving and blinded soul. How is that to be cured? There is but one way — unhappiness. There is so much that is seductive around you; so much worldly impressionability, so much perpetual fascination, all like so many successive layers covering over the inspirations of the soul, that misfortune, and misfortune only, can save you. God has often struck you down in His mercy. He has struck you in your heart, your affections, and your health; He has struck you when He permitted you to make certain discoveries about humanity, — discoveries which have made a deep impression on your heart, and rendered it insensible to the attractions of this world. A bandage has fallen from your eyes, and you seem to find yourself in a new world. That world which you knew before, or thought you knew, now appears to be a region of phantoms only, — of vain, deceitful, perfidious shadows. You are discouraged, but you are also cured, — cured of your illusions, and cured of that blindness which was perhaps leading you to the edge of a precipice. Thank God for it, but be careful never to return to that land of shadows, for they will always be the same they have been; they will caress you in order to betray you, and leave a poisoned dart in your heart while they embrace you. Walk with confidence in the new path which Providence has opened for you, for there you stand on the solid ground of truth and virtue.

I have already mentioned a sickness, which I shall call divine, a heavenly nostalgia; a weariness and disgust which sometimes takes possession of the heart on beholding the littleness and the miseries of this world, or else in consequence of a void which makes itself felt, we cannot tell why, in all our interior faculties. I entreat souls attacked by this divine illness, I implore of them, to profit of this disgust for earthly things, to loosen their bonds, and daily detach themselves more and more from this world and all its falsehood and frivolity.

But there is one danger here which I wish to point out, — that of indulging in a gloomy sadness, which is the very opposite of a right Christian spirit. The just soul, according to the beautiful expression of Bossuet, should ever find serenity on its lofty eminence, breathe there a fresher, purer air, and invest itself with the calm luminous tints of the firmament, in proportion as it ascends on high. When the heart is gloomy it has but to turn to God, and it becomes enlightened; when it is sad with one of those indefinable sadnesses which seem shapeless and baseless, the soul has but to remember God, and the peace of Heaven soon dissipates all clouds. " I remembered God and was delighted." [1]

There is one last grace of which I have not yet spoken, but of which I wish you to have at least a perception, — the grace of these our meetings, of this our association; were it only in consequence of those words of our Divine Saviour — " Where two or three are gathered together in my name, there am I in the

---

[1] Psalm lxxvi. 4.

midst of them." How often have I already prayed, how often shall I not pray, my children, for the grace to elevate your hearts more and more, until I can attach them to the vault of Heaven, chaining them there with the fetters of divine love, enveloping them in holy bonds, and then returning them to God, as a nurse returns her children to their real mother — "As if a nurse should cherish her children."[1] But you must come to my aid in this good work, my children; you must help me by your generous concurrence and your filial obedience, in order that you may be one day enabled to say, borrowing the words of the Apostle, "The grace of this association has not been made void in me." "And His grace in me hath not been void."[2]

---

[1] 1 Thess. ii. 7.   [2] 1 Cor. xv. 10.

21*

SIXTEENTH DISCOURSE.

ON GRACE.

CONTINUED.

"Neglect not the grace which is in thee."—1 TIM. iv. 14.

GOD could do everything for us without any effort on our part. He could command graces to increase and multiply, and produce fruit in us, without our own coöperation, as He commands the dew to refresh and fertilize the plants of the earth, and the plants to shoot and grow, and bear flowers and fruits, without possessing the power of resisting the necessary laws which govern their development. Our Lord has not willed that we should be treated in like manner, because we are rational beings, and the essence of love consists in being free and acting freely; and because it will tend more to our happiness and glory in Heaven to be able to say, as we look at our crown, I myself, with the help of God, have obtained this, and have adorned it with all those beauteous flowers, through my own diligence and efforts. God, then, desires our coöperation with the graces He sends us, as St. Leo says.[1] He desires that a free

---

[1] Serm. xxxv. vol. i. ch. iii. p. 251.

creature should correspond of its own free will with
the gifts of Heaven. He never imposes anything by
force on us. He asks the soul, Will you do this?
and if she refuse, He waits with patience. This
problem, so laid down, explains why so many men
are unbelievers. God is never wanting to a soul, but
souls are often wanting to Him. There are always
graces at the disposition of men; graces which might
impel them to the first upward tendency, graces of
the most intimate union with God; graces, in a word,
for the first and earliest efforts, as well as those for
the most eminent degrees of sanctity. But souls resist all these, and turn away from them, for they are
bound down with ropes which hold them back, and
are fixed to one spot under heavy anchors of iron.

God has two general laws which preside over the
distribution of His graces. First come the designs
of His providence, which orders everything for the
greater good and greater perfection of the universe,
and according to the rules of His wisdom and om-
nipotent will; and then the necessity of making allowances for the particular characteristics of each
being, for those who are best disposed will of course
receive most. St. Thomas would seem to have given
us a perfect summary of these two laws when he
writes — "Divine grace is undoubtedly infinite, and
can bestow itself without measure if the principle
only of its action be considered; but the effects grace
produces are in proportion to the capacity of those
creatures to whom it is given, and to the designs of
God."[1] In His relation to the working of that sec-

[1] 3a, p, q. 57, art. 3.

ond law, — that is to say, the law which has reference to the understanding of creatures, and which is the only one of which I am treating at the present moment, — God is like the sun, which pours forth its luminous rays with marvellous profusion, shedding them superabundantly on all His creatures with regard to everything concerning Himself, but in reality bestowing much more on pure transparent substances than on dark and earthy ones. Our Lord, like a torrent rushing forth impetuously from its source, pours out His benefits on all alike, and the cause of their unequal distribution lies solely in the minds of men.[1] Those who are well disposed, and endowed with a good understanding, receive much, and others less.[2] I picture to myself a large number of vessels of different sizes placed beside the seashore: the tide rises suddenly, and the advancing waves, in all their majesty and volume, fill up in an instant what was empty before. It is a matter of indifference to them to bestow much or little, the unequal size of the vessels being alone the cause of the unequal distribution.[3]

[1] What I say here refers solely to the supposition contained in the second law of Providence.

[2] It is in this sense Leibnitz says, "God is the source of perfection in the nature and the actions of His creatures ; but the limited capability of receiving which a creature possesses is the cause of the defects in its actions." — Essays on the Goodness of God, pt. i. n. 30.

[3] Let me quote some passages from the holy Doctors on this important point. I shall begin with St. Dionysius. "The Sovereign Goodness invites all creatures to participate in it according to the measure of each one's understanding." — De Cœl. Hier. ch. iv. sec. 1, vol. i. p. 178. "Things divine are proportionately revealed to each one." — De Divin. Nom. ch. i. sec. i. p. 587. "We will explain this

I.

First of all, you must promptly respond to the call of grace. Promptitude and fervor are among the qualities of true love. If you ask a friend to do you a favor, and if he instantly hastens to oblige you, although there is no necessity for his immediate services, you feel deeply touched and gratified. Why is this? Because, when love is true and, sincere, it gushes forth the moment it finds an opening. If you dig down through a mountain, or into a plain which

more clearly by means of examples which may assist our feeble understanding. The rays of the sun penetrate easily through that clear, transparent matter which it first meets, whence it issues full of lustre and brilliancy; but when it comes to fall on denser bodies, the very obstacle which these atoms naturally oppose to the diffusion of its light causes it to shine with a dull and sombre radiance, until fading away by degrees, it becomes almost invisible. . . . This law of the physical world is reproduced in the superior world." — De Hierar. Cœlest. ch. xiii. sec. i. p. 302. "Grace is susceptible of being measured or lessened in its relations to him who receives it, for one man may be more enlightened than another with this heavenly light ; the reason of this diversity lying partly in the preparation made for its reception, for he who more diligently prepares himself will obtain a greater abundance of grace." — St. Thomas, 1a, 2æ, q. 112, art. 4. "If grace," says St. Jerome, "be given within certain limits, it is not that God sets any bounds to His Divine Spirit and grace, because His munificence is infinite ; but that He only pours out that heavenly gift in proportion to the measure of capacity of the vessels destined to receive it. He gives only as much of His gifts to man as man can receive. The Spirit of God is not weighed by measure ; that which everywhere encompasses us has no limits. To make it still clearer, let us give another example. The sea is boundless, and its extent known only to God ; yet if you sought to distribute its waters among many, it is evident they would be unequally divided, according to the quantity each man had strength to carry away." — In Epist. ad Ephes. iv. 7, vol. vii. p. 497, edit. Migné.

contains water, it gushes out impetuously the moment you reach the reservoir, and your artesian well is complete. It is the same thing with the feelings of the heart, — they too manifest themselves in sudden, quick outbursts. On the other hand, here is a person who seems to be your friend, and as long as protestations only of friendship are required, he has a flow of words at his disposal; his fine speeches follow each other with the rapidity of steam. But one fine day you ask him to do you a favor which is quite within his power. He does not exactly say no, but he hesitates, and waits, and wavers, and seeks to make excuses, and finds there are a quantity of *ifs* and *buts* to be considered. He wishes you to believe that he is devoted to your interests, but that there are cases when one cannot act as one would wish. You quickly form your opinion of that person, and know then to what category he belongs.

Consider, also, for these comparisons appear to me serviceable in throwing light on this very practical subject, — consider, I say, that woman whom you have awakened at an early hour in the morning, but who is indolent, and, perhaps, even very lazy, and is always heavily asleep when she ought to be getting up. She opens her eyes only to shut them again, and turn round on the other side. There is such a tender friendship between her and her pillow, that she indulges herself in the pleasure of unspoken communion with it. She is still immovable, in an hour, two hours later; and it is only by a supreme effort that she can tear herself from her downy rest, made so dear to her by her indolent nature, and even that is accomplished with sighs worthy of some act of heroism. I can give you no better description of the state of some souls with relation to grace. Their sleep is equally profound, and their waking moments are followed by a still worse lethargy, so that their slumbers, though at times interrupted, lasts during their whole lifetime. Our Lord calls them; they look up, shake their heads, and sink still deeper into the depths of indifference. If the divine warning be persisted in, they turn their back on it, and feel inclined to say to our Lord that He is too importunate, and might at least let them sleep in peace. There are actually Christians, whose lives are thus passed in continued slumber, — a slumber at times broken and interrupted by the calls of our Saviour. Am I not now giving the true history of a soul, perhaps of more than one soul among my audience, whose secrets are known to God alone? Answer truly and conscientiously, soul so dear to God, and admit that He is constantly pursuing you with all the artifices of love. God has called to you for a long time past, He has knocked at your door, He has urged and entreated, and made use of everything on earth to draw you to Himself. You do not actually refuse His invitation, but you draw back and wait, and turn again on the pillow of spiritual sloth. You say to yourself — God requires too much of me; it is too soon. Of course I mean to obey Him, but to-morrow will be time enough. And the morrow, so often repeated, becomes — *never.*

If you wish to be pleasing to God, my children, do what He asks of you at once. That is the test of real love, and the sure means of making rapid progress in virtue. A sacrifice made for God, made instantly, with all the spontaneous ardor of affection, is of incalculable value in His sight, and saints have owed their perfection to that first act. You may think that a small sacrifice is but a little thing. I am not of the same opinion. A little sacrifice is often very important in itself, and in its consequences. And, even admitting your reasoning, I would still say — The sacrifice in itself may seem a little thing, but the love which has prompted it with such eagerness is very great; it is worth more than any and everthing else in life, and is the true riches of the heart. Besides, are you very sure that the sacrifice God demands is a small one? You try to persuade yourself and others that it is so, but is that the truth? Your delays are, perhaps, shallow excuses, which you put forward with the intention of their eventually becoming an absolute refusal; for you perfectly understand the extent of what God demands, but you hope to deceive Heaven as you would deceive a creditor whom you put off from day to day. Ah! let me implore of you not to cherish such vain illusions. Yield to God's power; give up your will to His immediately; resign all to Him before you leave this church. This instant immolation which I ask of you may have an important bearing on your future life. Our Lord once called to the young Samuel, in the middle of the night. Three times the same voice was heard, and three times Samuel rose instantly and sought the High Priest, and when he knew that it was God Who called, he said, "Speak, Lord, Thy

servant heareth," and is ready to obey. What an
admirable example of prompt correspondence with
grace? How many times, Christian souls, has God
spoken to you and called you by name, and you
heard the summons distinctly? I am not speaking
now of a voice heard by the ears of the body, for the
words of God generally take the form of interior
lights. When you hear those voices, my children, I
entreat of you to rise quickly, as Samuel did, and to
say, "O Lord, my God, behold me whom Thou hast
called. Speak, for Thy servant heareth, and is ready
to do all that Thou commandest." One single act of
this prompt, entire obedience, may be the first step
for you of that ladder whose topmost rung rests on
Heaven.

II.

The second quality of coöperation with grace is
generosity. Generosity is that tendency of the mind
which makes men not stop to calculate, but give
freely, and find pleasure in so giving. The man who
calculates has never really loved, and this saying
is most true with regard to our relations with God.
With creatures, it is often necessary to calculate and
take precautions, there are so few souls worthy of a
blind confidence; but with God there should be no
hesitation, no reserve. We should give ourselves to
Him entirely, unconditionally, and without any mental reservation. This is a beautiful and almost divine
offering, but, alas! too rare. One day I said to a
person, that she gave me the idea, in her conduct

to Almighty God, of a person standing on the water's brink, cautiously stepping in a little, yet fearing to quit the shore, and still clinging to the shrubs for help. You will gain nothing until, disengaging yourself from earth, you throw yourself boldly in and begin to swim. Yes, you must swim, and that, too, courageously. The comparison is a good one, for the swimmer is lightly clad, and clings to nothing, but ventures boldly into the great ocean.

Be generous with God, my children; true love is always generous. A selfish, calculating love is no better than tepid water, which turns the heart sick. O soul, so beloved of God, yet, perhaps, so faithless to Him, you complain of having made no progress in virtue, and seem to say, It is not my fault. Ah! what would you think of a child who could weigh its duty towards its parents, not committing, it is true, any grave offences, but who, apart from that, should give them the smallest possible amount of affection and tenderness, and should daily wound their hearts by a constant, calculated withholding of all kind and loving attentions? How would you answer that child, if it said, Is it my fault that I make no progress in filial piety, and that those cordial relations, which throw such a charm round other families, do not exist between my parents and me? Would you not reply, Unnatural child, can you not see that you yourself are destroying the little feeling of affection that is in you, by the slow poison you are pouring into it? It is a miracle if any still lives in you; and, on the other hand, do you not see that each of your words, acts, and proceedings, is a sort of icy moral

shower-bath, outpoured on your parents' hearts?
Christian soul, you have just pronounced your own
condemnation; you yourself are that unnatural child,
who calculates all that it does for God. You are
like the shopman, who measures his stuff with
miserly exactness, giving the least he can, and who
endeavors to retrench a few threads daily from the
right quantity. This is just what you do with God,
Who desires, on the contrary, that you should cut
your cloth largely, — that is, that He should be the
master of your thoughts and feelings. Say no longer
it is not your fault that you do not advance in virtue, for it is your fault, your grievous fault, and you
should strike your breast in sign of repentance, not
three times, but a hundred times.

We shall never repent, my children, of having
been generous to God. He is so good, He so earnestly desires our welfare, that we shall never regret
abandoning ourselves entirely to His guidance. He
never requires a sacrifice from us that is not for our
real happiness. It costs us something to do it, particularly in the beginning, though it should only be a
change of dress. It costs the seaman something,
too, to break through his home life, leave the harbor
behind, and sail elsewhere; but when once he is out
on the wide ocean, what a glorious expanse lies before him, what a joyous feeling of freedom. It costs
the laborer something to rise at dawn of day, and to
water the furrows of earth with the sweat of his
brow; but what a rich reward he has when the harvest comes. How he rejoices in that hour. Generosity often works a marvellous effect in the heart of

God; you shall be the judges of this yourselves. You have an enemy, to whom you feel a profound antipathy. You hear one day that this enemy of yours has just performed an act of great generosity towards you, that he has freely and willingly rendered you a great service, delivered you from a great danger, and done this even at the cost of a great sacrifice to himself. Straightway the ice of your heart is melted, and when you meet him in person you testify the warmest gratitude to him. This being the effect of a generous act on you, judge what must be its influence on the heart of a God Who so tenderly loves us. Generosity is love under the form of an elixir; and love, when fervent and earnest, can do what it will with God. Try the experiment for yourselves, my children. Let your heart belong unreservedly to God, act with entire confidence in Him, and have no debit and credit account with Him. If you received no other recompense on earth but love, you would be well paid, but in heaven that love will be returned to you a hundred fold.

III.

We must also correspond with grace by love. Transport yourselves in imagination into a large family, and you will see how all the children obey, but with very different feelings. The eldest one's heart is loving, therefore all that he does is animated and inspired by a deep affection. The second is also of a loving nature, but other less elevated considerations are mingled with it; the water, though pure, has some clayey matter in it. With the third, the love is still less, and partakes of a fear that is more or less servile; finally, the younger ones submit merely to avoid punishment, or not to lose their portion of the inheritance. It is needless to ask you which of those characters you prefer: your maternal hearts cannot and never do hesitate in their choice for a moment, for love has essential principles which cannot be transgressed with impunity. Then, as God is our Father, and love comes from Him, and the true laws by which it is governed here below flow from the source of all love, how can it be otherwise in its relations with God? One thought of pure and fervent love is more acceptable to Him than all possible bodily mortifications done with a less pure and fervent intention. One sigh of pure love, and a great sinner is pardoned. One instant of fervent love, of the concentrated essence of purest love, and the soul has attained the heights of perfection.

I cannot exhort you too earnestly, my children, to live that life of love even in the world: that life in which, as the saints say, everything that we say and do and think is quickened by the love of God, with some little differences, which are but on the exterior; and the soul resembles the bee which, in all its numerous flights through the country and in its harvest among the flowers, is solely occupied with making honey. You may think that these winged thieves, as St. Francis of Sales calls them, are pillaging the lily, the heather, and the wild thyme; but in one sense you are wrong, for though it is true they are hovering over the flowers, yet they are always storing their honey; that is ever their first and chief occupation. In the same way, you see a pious woman entirely devoted to the care of her household, to the love of her husband, of her children, and to good works for her neighbor, and you think these her sole occupations; and in a certain sense this is quite true, but in a still higher one she is making and storing the honey of the love of God. When you have attained to this most blessed state of being, you will continually perform deeds worthy of the angels, and you will perform them while presiding over your family meals, or directing the details of your household, or giving gladness by your delicate attentions and thoughtful foresight to your husband, children, and all who are connected with you. You see that it is not so difficult to win Heaven with a little energy; everything depends on the way you set about it.

You will also draw great advantage from following this method. "Grace," says St. Thomas, "enables us at last to do everything easily and naturally, and gives to all our actions ease, pleasure, and perfection."[1] Yes, love fervently and you will succeed; everything becomes easy and agreeable when the heart inspires it, for hearts are gifted with a steam-power, with which nothing can compare. If you serve God from fear, you are like a heavy steam-engine without fire — so weighty in its solid mass of iron that, if several men try to push it forward they can scarcely move it a few yards, and even that is effected in the most provokingly slow manner. But

---

[1] Cont. Gent. bk. iii. ch. cl.

watch it when it gets its steam up, when all its machinery is set in motion; the great wheels move round, and the engine rushes steadily forward in its course. 'Tis an image of the soul when animated with a fervent love! Try this experience for yourselves, my children, for with it and by the aid of grace all our actions may be performed with an ease and naturalness, a pleasure and propriety, which can never be imagined by the children of the world, nor by the timorous, ignorant souls for whom God's service is only a heavy yoke and burden.

IV.

The fourth condition of coöperation with grace is perseverance. Perseverance and steadfastness in well-doing are, again, some of the consequences of the love of God. I do not ask impossibilities; did I do so, I should be more severe with you than Almighty God is. I do not require that you should be without fault, that you should never fall into error; but what I *do* require is that you should have a persevering good will, a firm resolution of rising again after your falls. That you will commit many faults I feel convinced; you will fall again and again, and must be patiently waited for. You will often have relapses, the results of which may be of the greatest use to you if they serve to make you more humble, teaching and reminding you that you are only dust and ashes. But let the desire of rising again and returning to the path of virtue be always steadily imprinted on your heart, as the intention of reaching the harbor is the fixed idea of the pilot, in spite of the contrary winds that oppose him. We sometimes meet with good, kind souls, but as change-able as the winds, — even as the equinoctial winds. Their being to-day in the north is the reason why to-morrow, or perhaps this evening, they will be in the south. If they have made an appointment with you in the east, and you wish to see them, you had better go to the west. They are always in extremes; and if some fine morning they find themselves in the path of good, they try to overcome all obstacles at a single bound. I prefer souls who advance more slowly, but who never stop on the way. It is the story of the hare and the tortoise over again ; and though I would not take the tortoise as my model for progress, yet, if I had to choose between them, I should certainly prefer it to the brainless hare, who goes by fits and starts, loses his head, stops on the way, exhausts his strength in useless wanderings, and sometimes ends by never reaching the goal.

You may, perhaps, object to me, What can be done if one is naturally inconsistent? In the first place, I set aside the imagination ; for that power of the soul in some people is what is called an incompressible fluid, — that is to say, it can neither be laid hold of, nor stopped, nor restrained. The best thing to be done is to leave it alone, and not trouble yourself about it. When it is weary, and tired of its length-ened wanderings, it will return home of itself. I shall only speak of inconsistency of will, and point out the two principal means of giving it steadiness.

Do you see those moving sands on the sea-shore? How will you deprive them of that motion, and turn them into solid rock? Take some lime and water; mix them together until they blend and form a cement which will so unite the grains of sand, that they become a solid block of stone. In the same way, you can cement your soul with prayer and the Sacraments, with the good counsels and prudent advice of a wise director, until, by degrees, your fickle will grows steady and firm to resist all external influences.

The second means is not to put too heavy a burden on your will. When pillars are slender, you take care to make the roof light. The burdens of the will are, disquietude about the future, the duties which we shall have to undertake, and the disgust and weariness which lie in wait for us. Cast away all that is unnecessary in those burdens which you make for yourselves, and particularly those with regard to time. I would advise some minds to live and look forward not only from day to day, but also from hour to hour, yea, from one minute to the next. Let them say to themselves in the morning, — " Now, I can do all this very well till the middle of the day. When midday comes, let them make the same resolution till evening. If that be not sufficient, they can divide the day into smaller portions. The burden will then seem lighter, and more easily borne. You will see the wisdom of this counsel if you reflect that eternity does not exist for us; the present minute, or rather the present moment only, is at our disposal. It is always easy, with the help of God, to bear the burden of a moment; and besides, according to the beautiful words of Holy Writ, "The instructions of wisdom are never out of time." [1] And, "Then shall be the time of everything." [2]

The Scripture says that the grace of God is a Paradise of benediction. May I have been enabled to prove this truth clearly to you during the course of my instructions. May I, above all, have been enabled to inspire you with a lively and ardent desire of coöperating with grace! Then will your souls become a Paradise of delight, which will recall to you the Eden of old. "Grace is like a Paradise in blessings, and mercy remaineth for ever." [3]

---

[1] Ecclus. xxii. 6.   [2] Eccles. iii. 17.   [3] Ecclus. xl. 17.